SOCIAL DANCE

Steps to Success

Judy Patterson Wright, PhD
Dance Educator
Champaign, Illinois

Leisure Press
Champaign, IL

Library of Congress Cataloging-in-Publication Data

Wright, Judy Patterson, 1946-
    Social dance : steps to success / Judy Patterson Wright.
      p.   cm.
    ISBN 0-88011-449-5
    1. Ballroom dancing. I. Title.
    GV1751.W86 1992   91-31230
    793.3'3--dc20   CIP

ISBN: 0-88011-449-5

Copyright © 1992 by Leisure Press

All rights reserved. Except for use in a review, the reproduction or utilization of this work in any form or by any electronic, mechanical, or other means, now known or hereafter invented, including xerography, photocopying, and recording, and in any information storage and retrieval system, is forbidden without the written permission of the publisher.

Acquisitions Editor: Brian Holding; **Developmental Editors:** June I. Decker, PhD, John Robert King, and Holly Gilly; **Assistant Editors:** Elizabeth Bridgett, Dawn Levy, and Kari Nelson; **Copyeditor:** Wendy Nelson; **Proofreader:** Laurie McGee; **Production Director:** Ernie Noa; **Typesetters:** Kathy Boudreau-Fuoss, Marcia Wildhagen, and Julie Overholt; **Text Design:** Keith Blomberg; **Text Layout:** Denise Lowry; **Cover Design:** Jack Davis; **Cover Photo:** Wilmer Zehr; **Author Photo:** Jim Corley, B & W Photography; **Line Drawings:** Sharon Barner; **Footwork Diagrams:** Gretchen Walters; **Printer:** United Graphics

Instructional Designer for the Steps to Success Activity Series: Joan N. Vickers, EdD, University of Calgary, Calgary, Alberta, Canada.

Leisure Press books are available at special discounts for bulk purchase. Special editions or book excerpts can also be created to specification. For details, contact the Special Sales Manager at Human Kinetics.

Printed in the United States of America   15 14 13 12 11 10

Human Kinetics
Web site: http://www.humankinetics.com/

United States: Human Kinetics, P.O. Box 5076, Champaign, IL 61825-5076
1-800-747-4457
e-mail: humank@hkusa.com

Canada: Human Kinetics, 475 Devonshire Road, Unit 100, Windsor, ON N8Y 2L5
1-800-465-7301 (in Canada only)
e-mail: humank@hkcanada.com

Europe: Human Kinetics, P.O. Box IW14, Leeds LS16 6TR, United Kingdom
+44 (0)113-278 1708
e-mail: humank@hkeurope.com

Australia: Human Kinetics, 57A Price Avenue, Lower Mitcham, South Australia 5062
(08) 82771555
e-mail: humank@hkaustralia.com

New Zealand: Human Kinetics, P.O. Box 105-231, Auckland Central
09-523-3462
e-mail: humank@hknewz.com

Contents

CONCORDIA UNIVERSITY LIBRARY
PORTLAND, OR 97211

Series Preface

The Steps to Success Activity Series is a breakthrough in skill instruction through the development of complete learning progressions—the *steps to success*. These *steps* help students quickly perform basic skills successfully and prepare them to acquire advanced skills readily. At each step, students are encouraged to learn at their own pace and to integrate their new skills into the total action of the activity, which motivates them to achieve.

The unique features of the Steps to Success Activity Series are the result of comprehensive development—through analyzing existing activity books, incorporating the latest research from the sport sciences and consulting with students, instructors, teacher educators, and administrators. This groundwork pointed out the need for three different types of books—for participants, instructors, and teacher educators—were needed. Together these books constitute the Steps to Success Activity Series.

The *participant book* for each activity is a self-paced, step-by-step guide; learners can use it as a primary resource for a beginning activity class or as a self-instructional guide. The unique features of each *step* in the participant book include

- sequential illustrations that clearly show proper technique for all basic skills,
- helpful suggestions for detecting and correcting errors,
- excellent drill progressions with accompanying *Success Goals* for measuring performance, and
- a complete checklist for each basic skill for a trained observer to rate the learner's technique.

A comprehensive *instructor guide* accompanies the participant's book for each activity, emphasizing how to individualize instruction. Each *step* of the instructor's guide promotes successful teaching and learning with

- teaching cues (*Keys to Success*) that emphasize fluidity, rhythm, and wholeness,

- criterion-referenced rating charts for evaluating a participant's initial skill level,
- suggestions for observing and correcting typical errors,
- tips for group management and safety,
- ideas for adapting every drill to increase or decrease the difficulty level,
- quantitative evaluations for all drills (*Success Goals*), and
- a complete test bank of written questions.

The series textbook, *Instructional Design for Teaching Physical Activities*, explains the *steps to success* model, which is the basis for the Steps to Success Activity Series. Teacher educators can use this text in their professional preparation classes to help future teachers and coaches learn how to design effective physical activity programs in school, recreation, or community teaching and coaching settings.

After identifying the need for participant, instructor, and teacher educator texts, we refined the *steps to success* instructional design model and developed prototypes for the participant and the instructor books. Once these prototypes were fine-tuned, we carefully selected authors for the activities who were not only thoroughly familiar with their sports but also had years of experience in teaching them. Each author had to be known as a gifted instructor who understands the teaching of sport so thoroughly that he or she could readily apply the *steps to success* model.

Next, all of the participant and instructor manuscripts were carefully developed to meet the guidelines of the *steps to success* model. Then our production team, along with outstanding artists, created a highly visual, user-friendly series of books.

The result: The Steps to Success Activity Series is the premier sports instructional series available today. The participant books are the best available for helping you to become a master player, the instructor guides will help you to become a master teacher, and the teacher educator's text prepares you to design your own programs.

This series would not have been possible without the contributions of the following:

- Dr. Joan Vickers, instructional design expert,
- Dr. Rainer Martens, Publisher,
- the staff of Human Kinetics Publishers, and

- the *many* students, teachers, coaches, consultants, teacher educators, specialists, and administrators who shared their ideas—and dreams.

Judy Patterson Wright
Series Editor

This book is written for beginning social dance students who want to know how to partner-dance in recreational (rather than competitive) dance settings, and for those who want the challenge of going beyond the traditional, ''packaged'' dance steps.

The purpose of this book is to simplify for beginning dancers what is usually perceived to be a complex, difficult process. My experience with traditional methods of teaching social or ballroom dance, and my research on the process of acquiring sequential skills, motivated me to produce a course with a different approach. The uniqueness of this approach to teaching social dance is its complete learning progression, which places skills and concepts along a continuum with uniquely designed practice drills for each learning step.

The sequence of learning steps in this book provides clear guidelines not only for how to execute the traditional basic steps for five different ballroom dances—swing, cha-cha, fox-trot, polka, and waltz—but also for how they are derived from everyday locomotor movements, how they are typically combined, how to decide when to use various dance-step options on the dance floor to best fit the flow of traffic, and how to create your own dance steps, combinations, sequences, or routines. Each basic dance is thoroughly explained and illustrated for both partners. Styling characteristics are explained with each dance style and applied in the drills. A list of abbreviations and a glossary are included for easy reference.

All of the previous skills depend upon knowing when to begin with the music, how to match your footwork to the tempo of the music, and how to move in unison with your partner in a repetitive, rhythmic, and fluid manner—abilities that are usually left to the students to practice on their own. However, these timing skills are critical foundational skills, and they are built into the early step progressions in two ways: (a) in the text descriptions and drills (see Step 2); and (b) in cross-references to the sample music located on the soundsheet inserted in this book. The soundsheet has a perforated edge, plays at 33-1/3 rpm, and the square sides of the soundsheet allow it to hug a turntable, especially when you place a phonograph record underneath it.

There are two basic options for using this book. The ideal procedure is to follow the steps (chapters) in order, to learn all five dance styles. However, if you have a particular interest in certain dance styles, or if you have limited time, you can complete Steps 1 through 3, and overview Steps 4 and 5 to select the styles you want to learn, follow your selected choices within Step 6, and complete the appropriate variation and combination options. In either case, if you follow the learning progressions in this book, you will soon find yourself pleasantly surrounded by others, enjoying their company, being challenged, and improving your fitness—all at the same time.

I wish to acknowledge the contributions of my many hundreds of students, who taught me as much as I taught them. I am grateful to Dr. Rainer Martens and Dr. Susan Wilmoth Savage for their encouragement to write down my ideas. I want to thank Dr. June Decker and Robert King, my developmental editors, for their helpful suggestions and guidance, and Holly Gilly, who helped put the finishing touches on this book. I also want to thank Dr. Margaret Thompson, Dr. Beverly Mackes, and Barbara Mechtly for their insightful review comments. I appreciate the long hours spent posing for the photographs used for the illustrations in this book by my models, Robert King, Jennie King, Valerie Hall, and Brad Colson. I also thank Richard Gardzina for the wonderful, original music used on the soundsheet.

I especially want to thank my husband, Sam, for being my dance partner in life as well as on the dance floor—he is definitely my ''Mr. Wright.'' Lastly, I dedicate this book to my parents, who have always encouraged me to be the best that I can be.

Judy Patterson Wright

The Steps to Success Staircase

Get ready to climb a staircase—one that will lead you to become an accomplished dancer. You cannot leap to the top; you get there by climbing one step at a time.

Each of the 12 steps you will take is an easy transition from the one before. The first few steps of the staircase provide a solid foundation of basic skills and concepts to help you understand alignment, musical structure, and coincidence anticipation (matching your footwork with the music). As you progress further, you will learn how to execute basic steps, communicate (verbally and nonverbally) with your partner, lead and follow, move from one dance position to another, combine dance variations into sequences, adapt your sequences to avoid collisions with other couples, and create your own dance sequences. As you near the top of the staircase, you will become more confident in your ability to be successful in five different dance styles—swing, cha-cha, fox-trot, polka, and waltz.

Familiarize yourself with this section as well as the ''Why Social Dance?'' section for an orientation and to understand how to set up your practice sessions around the steps.

Follow the same sequence each step (chapter) of the way:

1. Read the explanations of what is covered in the step, why the step is important, and how to perform or apply the items focused on in the step, which may be basic skills, concepts, variations, or options.
2. Follow the Keys to Success illustrations showing exactly how to position your body to execute each basic skill successfully. There are three general parts to each skill: preparation phase (starting position), execution phase (performing the skill that is the focus of the step), and styling phase (adding characteristic style, smoothness, and consistency).
3. Be aware of the common errors that may occur and the recommendations for how to correct them.
4. The drills help you improve your skills through repetition and purposeful practice. Read the directions and the Success Goal for each drill. Practice accordingly, and record your scores. Compare your score with the Success Goal for the drill. For each dance style, you need to meet the Success Goal of each drill before moving on to practice the next one, because the drills are arranged in an easy-to-difficult progression. This sequence is designed specifically to help you achieve continual success.
5. As soon as you can reach all the Success Goals for one step, you are ready for a qualified observer—such as your teacher, coach, or trained partner—to evaluate not only your basic skill technique but also your ability to demonstrate the appropriate styling characteristics according to the Keys to Success Checklist. This qualitative or subjective evaluation is important because using correct form and styling can enhance your performance. Your evaluator can tailor specific goals for you, if they are needed, by using the Individual Program form (see Appendix).
6. Repeat these procedures for each of the 12 Steps to Success. Then rate yourself according to the directions in the ''Rating Your Total Progress'' section at the end of the book.

Good luck on your step-by-step journey to developing your social dancing skills, building confidence, experiencing success, and having fun!

Key

CW = Clockwise

CCW = Counterclockwise

LOD = Line of direction

L = Left

R = Right

O.F. = Original front

⟶ = Direction of movement

= Woman's footwork (right foot shaded)

= Man's footwork (right foot shaded)

= Foot prepares to move

= Weight on ball of foot

Why Social Dance?

Throughout history, our social needs have been reflected in our dance forms. These social needs were first displayed in primitive courtship and tribal dances. Although primitive dances were often performed by members of the same sex with no bodily contact, social dance is essentially touch dancing and includes all forms of partner dancing done primarily for recreation or pleasure to a variety of musical styles.

The sometimes synonymously used term *ballroom dance* refers to partner dances done in a ballroom to traditional ballroom music. The earliest eighteenth- and nineteenth-century forms of ballroom dance were the minuet in France, and quadrille (a two-, four-, or more, couple dance) in France and England, the waltz in Austria, and the polka in France. It became fashionable during the Renaissance for ladies and gentlemen of the court to dress well and have polished manners. Soon, competition to outdo others led to elaborate balls and the hiring of dance masters to teach peasant dances to the aristocracy.

Additional partner dances done for pleasure and recreation were introduced early in the twentieth century, including the fox-trot, lindy, two-step, tango, samba, rhumba, and cha-cha. After World War II, traditional ballroom dancing and music went into a decline, but partner dancing continued in popularity throughout the rock-and-roll era and was perpetuated by the romantic disco era. A revival in partner dancing continues to the present day—mainly due to the attractive benefits of social dancing!

BENEFITS OF SOCIAL DANCE

The foremost reason for participating in partner or touch dancing is the sheer joy of moving rhythmically in unison with a partner to music—regardless of your age. Being with a partner not only enhances the pleasure, but also highlights the social benefits, of meeting others (sometimes with romance in mind). Many married couples have first met on the dance floor—including my husband and me! Through dancing, partners can share common interests, learn to respect each other's rights, and show appreciation for each other's efforts.

An added benefit of ballroom dancing is being in pleasant, unstressful surroundings (large ballrooms) that emphasize proper etiquette and attire, which can be mentally refreshing. Listening to music is often very relaxing. Even if you are not dancing in a ballroom, you can be more in touch with your body and partner (be in the present) and, thus, less likely to worry about day-to-day events (either past or future).

A third major benefit of participating in partner dancing is the low-impact aerobic workout you receive by dancing continuously. Partner dancing is a great way to blend exercise and recreation because you can raise your heart rate up to 60 to 70 percent of its maximum, which boosts stamina safely. All you have to do to achieve aerobic benefit is gradually increase the amount of time you dance continuously. Start by dancing the length of one song, and gradually add more time until you are dancing 15 to 60 minutes nonstop, three times per week.

Lastly, you can experience great personal satisfaction from your accomplishments in dancing—including improved posture, coordination, balance, precision, timing, and concentration. Additional satisfaction comes from knowing how to ask a partner to dance (or how to accept a dance), how to lead (or follow), and how to adapt your variations to fit the traffic flow of other couples.

SOCIAL DANCE TODAY

Numerous opportunities exist for recreational dancing. These include proms, cotillions, military balls, wedding receptions, and dances sponsored by schools, universities, colleges, parks, clubs, communities, and dance studios.

If you have the interest, you may also opt to dance on a competitive level. Competition may range from performing for yourself or others (the drills in Step 12 will help you explore some of these possibilities). Another performing option is to create a dance formation team—a group of two or more couples who constantly move from one formation to another (as does a marching band) as they dance.

Lastly, the United States Amateur Ballroom Dancers Association (USABDA) also stresses the physical, mental, and social benefits of ballroom dancing as a *lifetime* activity. Recently, they aired on PBS a program titled "Ballroom Dancing—The Sport of the 90's," which caused hundreds of interested inquiries. Try to watch the annual ballroom championships aired on PBS. After you finish this book, you will certainly be more appreciative of these dancers' stamina and expertise. For information on USABDA membership and additional dance opportunities, contact National Secretary, USABDA, 8102 Glen Gary Road, Baltimore, MD, 21234, 1-800-447-9047.

Step 1   Body Alignment and Carriage

Before you begin to dance, you need to get into the proper frame of mind—and body. This means forgetting about all of the everyday tasks that need to be done and problems that need to be solved. Think of shutting a door to the rest of your world, and focus on your body.

Now, how are you sitting or standing? Are you slumped forward or leaning back? Are your feet flat on the floor? Is your lower back straight or excessively arched? Are you standing with your weight all on one leg? In other words, are you demonstrating correct posture? The purpose of Step 1 is to increase your awareness of correct body posture, which is called *alignment* if you are standing stationary, and *carriage* if you are moving.

WHY ARE BODY ALIGNMENT AND CARRIAGE IMPORTANT?

Have you ever noticed how good dancers make their movements look easy? The illusion of ease is created by their standing body posture, carriage, styling, and fluidity. Their mistakes are often unnoticed, because they keep moving. They connect individual dance steps into continuous, pleasing sequences—never once looking at their feet!

Your body is your instrument of expression. To dress neatly and maintain proper body alignment is to give an impression to the world that you feel good about yourself. Proper body alignment allows you to use your muscles most efficiently, with the least amount of effort or extra muscular tension. Your standing posture is the standard to which you add the various dance stylings, or characteristics that commonly describe particular dances. For example, the waltz has a subtle rise-and-fall motion, and the swing (also called the *lindy)* has torso leans and syncopation. It is critical to correct any deviations in standing posture,

because they will be magnified tenfold when you move.

HOW TO EXECUTE PROPER BODY ALIGNMENT AND CARRIAGE

Correct posture is usually thought to be something like the weather: Everyone talks about it, but what can you do about it? You, too, may have fallen into the habit of taking posture for granted. However, now is the time to check your posture. Visualization techniques are particularly effective ways to learn how to correctly align your body. Try both of the following images. Which helps you visualize proper vertical alignment? Perhaps other images come to mind.

First, stand with your hands at your sides, with your feet no more than shoulder-width apart and your knees slightly bent. As if you are balancing large blocks on top of one another, place your hips, shoulders, and head directly above your feet. Look forward with your head erect (it is helpful to look at an object that is at eye level). Think of both shoulders being pulled down and back, which brings your shoulder blades closer together. Contract your abdominals and lengthen (rather than arch) your lower back. You are now in proper standing alignment.

Another way to check your alignment is to imagine a plumb line (a string suspended from the ceiling with a weight on it) hanging at your side. Adjust your posture so that your ear, shoulder, hip, knee, and ankle align with the string. Again, check that your shoulders are back, your abdominals are firm, and your lower back is long (not curved sharply or hyperextended). Figure 1.1 shows the proper standing alignment.

The previous vertical images are helpful when you are stationary. However, once you begin moving, you need to think of three-dimensional images that might help you maintain this correct alignment. For example, visualize your body as a suit of clothing (without wrinkles). Or imagine that a series of coiled bedsprings (at your neck, waist, arms, and legs) connect your head and your upper and lower torso over your feet.

Figure 1.1 Keys to Success: *Body Alignment and Carriage*

Preparation Phase (Alignment)

1. Center weight over feet ____
2. Align body segments using imagery ____
3. Head upright, eyes level ____
4. Pull shoulders back, down ____
5. Lower back long ____
6. Abdomen firm ____
7. Knees slightly bent ____

Execution Phase (Carriage)

1. Maintain vertical alignment ____
2. Fluid movements ____
3. Transfer weight onto balls of feet ____

Detecting Errors in Body Alignment and Carriage

Again, any alignment errors in standing posture are greatly magnified when you move, which will detract from your dancing style. Also be aware of any tendency to watch your feet or the floor. These problems usually fade once you have become able to align properly without conscious effort and have memorized the basic steps. Making a postural change will take frequent and daily self-reminders for almost 6 months. Select only one error at a time to correct, and be persistent—you can succeed! Typical standing errors and corrections are listed below.

ERROR

CORRECTION

1. Head is forward, with eyes focused downward.

1. Look at a point that is at your eye level, such that an imaginary line from your eyes to that point would be parallel to the floor (see Figure 1.1). You can pick out a specific crack or line on the wall in front of you, or, if necessary, place a piece of tape on the wall at your eye level. Notice that your spot corresponds to your height.

2. Lower back is curved too much, with hips back and abdomen forward.

2. You need to (a) increase your lower back flexibility as well as (b) strengthen your abdominal muscles. Both problems can be corrected by doing exercises at home, lying on your back with your knees bent, feet flat on the floor, and arms at your sides. For flexibility, try a pelvic tilt. Concentrate on contracting your abdominals, tilting your pelvis to gently press your lower back to the floor. For strength, try a low-intensity sit-up. Tuck your chin, contract your abdominals, and slowly lift your shoulders off the floor. Keep arms folded across your chest. As you lower, slowly press each vertebra down.

ERROR

CORRECTION

3. Body weight is back on heels.

3. Follow the directions in Drill 1 (in the next section) to become more aware of how to center your weight and to let it move forward over the balls of your feet. This is a ready position in sports.

Body Alignment and Carriage Drills

1. From a Balanced to a Ready Position

a. Review Figure 1.1a to get a mental image of correct standing alignment. Then stand and close your eyes. Experiment to find your balance or center point by deliberately moving your center of gravity (hips and torso) slightly beyond your base of support (your feet), and catch yourself before you actually fall. Notice how stable or unstable it feels when you let your center of gravity do the following:

   • Rock forward over your toes
   • Rock backward over your heels
   • Lean to your right side
   • Lean to your left side
   • Balance your weight (between your toes, heels, and sides of feet)

b. With your eyes open, repeat a. From your balanced position, allow your weight to move slightly forward over the balls of your feet. This is a ready position that permits you to move quickly in any direction (see Figure 1.1b). For the remainder of this book, you will constantly be moving into a ready position.

Success Goals = 10 repetitions of correct alignment (a) in a balanced position (with eyes closed), then (b) in a ready position (with eyes open)

Your Score =

   a. (#) ____ repetitions to a balanced position (eyes closed)

   b. (#) ____ repetitions to a ready position (eyes open)

2. *Direction Possibilities*

The purpose of this drill is to highlight the fact that movement is possible in eight directions— all relative to the direction you are facing in your original starting position.

To start, select one wall to face, which will be your starting position, or original front (O.F) for this drill. Stand in proper alignment with shoulders squared and parallel to your O.F. wall. Rock your body weight slightly forward to get into your ready position.

Ask a partner to call out the following directions for you to move in. After you hear the direction, walk four steps in the appropriate direction and walk four steps back to your original starting position. (Keep your shoulders parallel with your O.F. except on the diagonals. Then angle your shoulders to face either your diagonal left or right front.) Try to keep your walking steps consecutive and fluid, while demonstrating proper carriage.

These are the eight possible movement directions for dance:

- Forward
- Backward
- Right (R)
- Left (L)
- Diagonal front (L or R)
- Diagonal back (L or R)

After you have walked in all eight directions, switch roles with your partner to repeat this drill.

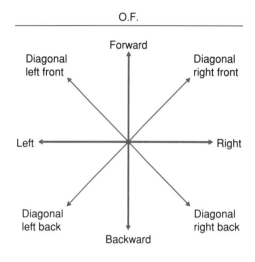

Success Goal = 2 repetitions of the walking sequence in the 8 directions with proper carriage

Your Score = (#) _____ repetitions of the walking sequence in the 8 directions with proper carriage

3. *Mind/Body Connection*

There is a reciprocal relationship between your mind and your body. Your attitude greatly affects your alignment and carriage, and vice versa.

When you are alone, concentrate on and act out any two of the following situations that will allow you to contrast extreme movement qualities, such as strong versus weak, light versus heavy, slow versus quick, sharp versus dull, and so forth:

- A tired, limp, lifeless position (standing or sitting)
- A butterfly moving
- A mule kicking
- A karate match with an invisible opponent
- Walking on ice
- Walking regally
- Displaying happiness
- Displaying sadness

Alternately assume opposing postures and contrast each quality for 60 seconds. Do you feel weaker or stronger after a particular one? Which one?

Success Goal = 60 seconds of alternately contrasting 2 qualities of movement (e.g., weak versus strong), identifying characteristics needed to create the illusions (e.g., of strength versus weakness)

Your Score = (#) _____ seconds of contrasting the two qualities

Weak postures are characterized by _____

Strong postures are characterized by _____

Answers: Weak postures and movements are characterized by unstable bases of support (e.g., standing with feet together, on one foot, on tiptoe), which projects a ''pushover'' or ''lightweight'' image. Strong postures and movements are characterized by stable bases of support (e.g., standing with feet apart and flat on floor, with knees bent), which project a strong, immovable image.

If you are feeling weak, you can reverse your mood and outlook by miming some strong situations. For example, repeat karate-type punches and kicks for 3 to 5 minutes. These sharp, staccato, controlled actions can help you feel stronger.

Body Alignment and Carriage
Keys to Success Checklist

Proper body alignment and carriage create an impression—literally an image for others that can either enhance or detract from your performance. It is important to have your posture evaluated by your teacher or another trained observer, both when you are standing and when you are moving. Stand sideways in your best posture, and ask your evaluator to place a checkmark by each item from Figure 1.1 that is observed. Then begin walking in a counterclockwise (CCW) direction, as your evaluator again evaluates and checks off those items observed.

If you have any postural deviations while standing, do they also appear as you are moving? If so, begin a daily self-check of your postural alignment—which may need to be repeated up to 30 times a day—until you have a strong mental image of vertical alignment. With practice, your posture and carriage will become more automatic.

Step 2 Understanding Musical Structure

A frequently asked question is "How do I know when to start moving with the music?" To those with a musical background or who have played an instrument or participated in other rhythmical activities, the answer to this question seems obvious, yet it is a critical and difficult question to answer if you have not had any rhythmical experiences. The purpose of this step (chapter) is twofold: (a) to identify musical cues, such as the number of beats per measure and the duration of the beats (the time signature), and the count(s) accented, for five social dances (the swing, cha-cha, fox-trot, polka, and waltz); and (b) to refine your discrimination of these musical cues so that you can identify which dance music is being played. All of the drills enhance your perceptual skills. These perceptual skills are critical preparation for learning how to coordinate your footwork to the music in Step 3.

WHY IS IT IMPORTANT TO RECOGNIZE MUSICAL STRUCTURES?

All music has rhythm. Rhythm is found everywhere—in everything from the sound of rain dropping on a roof, to symmetrical architectural designs (with repeating curves and balanced window placements) and asymmetrical architectural design (with starting and stopping patterns and unbalanced window placements), to the rhythmical structure of music. The challenge is to become aware of these possible rhythmic patterns and cues; they can help you identify the appropriate music for a particular dance and, later, coordinate your footwork with the music and select an appropriate dance step to match the music.

The advantage of understanding musical structures is that you will be able to answer the following questions:

- How many beats occur per measure?
- Why are accents used?
- When do I start? (On the downbeat? On the upbeat?)
- How fast should I move?
- Which dance music is being played?

HOW TO RECOGNIZE MUSICAL STRUCTURE

If you are mathematically inclined, you will appreciate the hierarchical relationships among musical notes. But even if you are not mathematically inclined, there is an order and consistency in music—it is not random. You need only to be able to recognize and identify that order and consistency.

Most social dance music has identifiable beats that can be grouped in multiples of 2 or 3 to create regular, recurring measures. On sheet music, vertical bars separate the beats into small groups called measures. These beats per measure are called the underlying beats, or beats for short. Without measures to separate and group the beats, there would not be an underlying rhythmic pattern to follow, because the beats would visually appear to be continuous—without any clear starting or stopping points (see Figure 2.1). However, just as you can see a measure on sheet music, you will be able to hear a measure in music that's being played, once you know both the number and duration of beats occurring per measure.

— — — — — — — — — — — — —

Figure 2.1 Continuous beats without measures.

The number and duration of beats per measure depend upon the time signature of the music. Common time signatures in social dance music include the fractional signs 2/4, 3/4, and 4/4. The numerator indicates the number of beats per measure, and the denominator indicates the duration of a particular beat. For example, the numerator values in Figure 2.2 signify that there are, respectively, 2, 3, and 4 beats per measure. The denominator value, 4, signifies that each quarter note in each example gets one count (one beat). In social dance music, it is safe to assume that the denominator will be 4, which means that each beat (each quarter note) gets one count. The number of beats per measure will be constant, with each underlying beat getting one count, for both the length and tempo of a particular song.

HOW TO DETERMINE THE NUMBER OF BEATS PER MEASURE

The easiest way to identify the number of beats per measure is to count in multiples of either 3 or 4 (the most common numerators). First try counting with the music in sets of four (1-2-3-4, 1-2-3-4, . . .). If your counts do not match the beats of the music, switch to counting in threes. One or the other will match. You may need to close your eyes to reduce outside distractions and focus all your attention on the music. One exception, the polka, has a 2/4 time signature, yet because the tempo is so fast, it is often easier to group your counts in fours. Thus, you can either memorize the fact that 2/4 time fits only polka music or use the general rule already mentioned. To test yourself on this general rule, complete Drill 1 (at the end of Step 2) now.

Another way to identify the number of beats per measure is to listen for accents. A beat or sound can be accented, or made to stand out, by making it either longer or stronger. In social dance music, certain accents are used within a measure that can alert you to what type of dance music is being played. If, for example, the first count is stronger than Counts 2 and 3, then a 3/4 time signature is being used, which is waltz music. If both Count 2 and Count 4 are stronger, then a 4/4 time signature is being used, which is either fox-trot or swing music. If Counts 3-and-4* are heaviest within a 4/4 time signature, then cha-cha music is being played. To test your recognition of accents, complete Drill 2 (at the end of Step 2) now.

A third way to identify the number of beats per measure is to listen for the bass players' or drummer's sounds rather than the melody. The melody is superimposed above the underlying beats and is variable, whereas the drum and other bass instruments regularly play the underlying beats, giving you more constant cues to follow.

HOW TO DETERMINE WHEN TO BEGIN

By the time you have heard the introduction and determined the number of beats per measure, the song is in progress. At that point, you can begin on the first count of any measure (the *downbeat*), begin on the first count of any phrase, or use some combination of the downbeats and the phrases. Most dancers use the third option.

A phrase is composed of two or more measures grouped together. For example, in a 4/4 time signature, if you group two measures

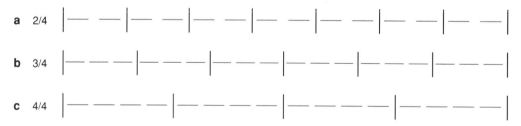

Figure 2.2 Underlying beats per measure for 2/4 time (a), 3/4 time (b), and 4/4 time signatures (c).

*Because the American version of the cha-cha is easier and faster to learn, it is described here. As you become more experienced, you can learn the Latin version, which has accents on Counts 4-and-1.

of four underlying beats together, you have an 8-count phrase. You can continue to group measures to get larger phrases. Thus, two 8-count phrases (four measures) combine to form a 16-count phrase. Two 16-count phrases (eight measures) combine to form a 32-count phrase, and so forth (see Figure 2.3).

In a 3/4 time signature, if you group two measures of three underlying beats together, you have a 6-count phrase. Two 6-count phrases (four measures) combine to form a 12-count phrase. Two 12-count phrases (eight measures) combine to form a 24-count phrase, and so forth (see Figure 2.4).

The arrows in Figures 2.3 and 2.4 indicate the first count (the downbeat) of each measure, or of each phrase grouping, for both 4/4 and 3/4 time signatures. Obviously, you have more chances of finding the downbeat by counting in measures. However, if you can also identify the beginning or end of a phrase, you'll get an additional cue as to when the next downbeat will occur.

Except for the polka, all of the dances covered in this book begin on the downbeat. The polka begins prior to Count 1 (on the *upbeat*). In this book, the upbeat is counted as an ''and.'' To test your ability to identify the downbeat and upbeat, complete Drill 3 (at the end of Step 2) now.

HOW TO DETERMINE THE TEMPO

How fast should you move? Typically, there are three different speeds or tempos used in social dance music: slow, moderate, and fast. Tempo will vary between songs, but it will always be constant within a particular song. Thus, once you have identified the speed, you can repeat that speed or tempo for the length of that song. To test your ability to identify the typical social dance tempos, complete Drill 4 (at the end of Step 2) now.

HOW TO DETERMINE WHICH MUSIC STYLE IS BEING PLAYED

Until this point, you have focused your attention mainly on identifying the number of beats

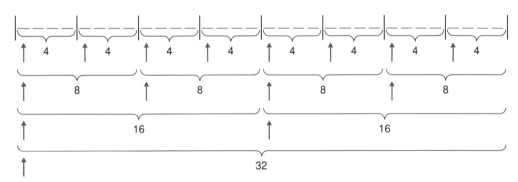

Figure 2.3 Phrase hierarchy for 4/4 time, with downbeats marked by arrows.

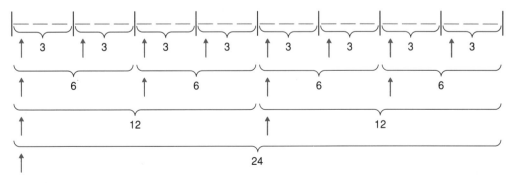

Figure 2.4 Phrase hierarchy for 3/4 time, with downbeats marked by arrows.

per measure, the time signature, and the counts accented—because they are consistent cues that must be identified early. Now you are ready to focus your attention on how the melody or lyrics of a song interacts with these constant cues.

The melody or lyrics provides an overlying rhythmic pattern superimposed on the underlying beats. The melody does not provide reliable rhythm cues, because it does not have to correspond exactly to the number of beats per measure, nor does it have to exactly fit one measure. However, particular styling cues that are characteristic of certain music are introduced through the melody or overlying rhythmic patterns.

To get a general idea of the unique styling for each of the five dances covered in this book, complete Drill 5 (at the end of Step 2) now.

Additional cues related to how you should move to the music are found by listening for the intensity, or amount of force exerted, in general within the music. For example, if you identify qualities in the music such as loudness, softness, heaviness, lightness, or sharpness, then you know what style of movements best accompany the music. To test yourself on recognizing different qualities of music, complete Drills 6 and 7 (at the end of Step 2) now.

Musical Structure Drills

Locate the soundsheet bound in this book, and gently remove it at its perforated edge. The soundsheet is designed to play at 33-1/3 rpm, and its square corners hug a turntable. For best results, place a phonograph record underneath the soundsheet. Thus, you will need a record player capable of 33-1/3 rpm and a phonograph record. All of the drills in Step 2 refer to the songs and song segments on this soundsheet. Feel free to listen as many times as necessary to answer the questions posed. Correct answers are provided at the end of the following drills.

1. Identify Beats per Measure

As you listen to the four song segments on Band 1, Side A, of the soundsheet, use the same procedure each time: (a) Listen for the pause at the end of the introduction, then (b) experiment with counting in either threes or fours. Remember that songs' introductions can vary in length and may or may not be representative of the measures to follow.

List how many beats per measure there are in each of the four song segments. These numbers represent the numerator in the time signature. You also know the time signature, because in social dance music a quarter note typically has one beat. Just add a 4 in the denominator. Fill in the time signature for each of the four song segments, too.

Success Goal = Correctly identify the number of beats per measure and the time signature for the 4 song segments on Band 1, Side A

Your Score =

Song Segment	Number of Beats/Measure	Time Signature
1		
2		
3		
4		

2. Identify Accents

Listen to the five song segments on Band 2, Side A. Identify the beat or beats that are stronger or heavier (accented). Basically, you have only three accent choices: Count 1, Counts 2 and 4, or Counts 3-and-4. Which best fits the music for each of these five song segments?

Success Goal = Correctly identify the accented count(s) for the 5 song segments

Your Score =

Song Segment	Count(s) Accented
1	
2	
3	
4	
5	

3. Identify the Downbeat/Upbeat

Again listen to the four song segments on Band 1, Side A, to identify which one begins on the upbeat. The other song segments begin on the downbeat. Either verbally or mentally count with an ''and'' between all whole counts: and-1-and-2-and-3-and-4, and so forth.

Success Goal = Correctly select the song segment that begins on the upbeat

Your Score = Song segment # _____ begins on the upbeat

4. Identify Tempos

Listen to the three song segments on Band 4, Side A. Compare and record the speed or tempo (slow, moderate, fast) of each song segment. Also, notice that each song segment has four beats per measure (4/4 time signature), has accents on Counts 2 and 4, and represents swing dance selections.

Success Goal = Correctly identify the tempo of each of the 3 song segments on Band 4, Side A

Your Score =

Song Segment	Tempo
1	
2	
3	

5. Identify Dance Styles

There are two parts to this drill. The first part reviews the previous drills, and the second part identifies characteristics associated with the five different types of dance music used in this book.
   a. Again listen to the five song segments on Band 2, Side A, and identify the number of beats per measure, the time signature, and the song segment that begins on the upbeat. Record your answers below.

Success Goal = Correctly identify the number of beats per measure, time signature, and the segment that begins on the upbeat from the five song segments on Band 2, Side A

Your Score =

Song Segment	Number of Beats/Measure	Time Signature	Begins on Upbeat
1			
2			
3			
4			
5			

   b. Again listen to the first two selections on Band 2, Side A, which are fox-trot and swing selections in 4/4 time. You may have difficulty distinguishing these song segments, because they both accent Counts 2 and 4. However, notice that the styles are slightly different; the fox-trot is smoother, whereas the swing is typically livelier and more syncopated. Keep in mind that these distinctions are easier to note with slow fox-trot tempos. If moderate- to fast-tempo fox-trots are played, it is very difficult to distinguish the fox-trot from the swing, unless the dance names are announced or listed. But don't worry! It is very common to see some dancers doing fox-trot and others doing swing steps to the same music, depending on the tempo. Ultimately, the choice will be yours—you'll need only to avoid bumping into anyone else. Continue to listen to these selections until you can notice the differences.

Now listen to and compare the remaining three song segments on Band 2, Side A. The third song segment is waltz music. The waltz selection is the easiest to follow, because it is the *only* example in 3/4 time. Listen for the characteristic accent (the stronger count) on the first count of each measure, followed by two lighter counts. This music is very smooth and flowing.

The fourth song segment on Band 2, Side A, is cha-cha music, which has a Latin quality and is in 4/4 time. Notice the heavier accents on Counts 3-and-4.

The fifth song segment is polka music. The polka is very quick and lively, with the accent on Count 1. Remember, it is in 2/4 time. (Yet sometimes it helps to count it in fours when you are learning to repeat the polka basic step on both sides.)

Success Goal = Correctly recognize 5 different types of dance music

Your Score = (#) _____ different types of dance music correctly recognized

6. *Identify Music Qualities*

Listen to the two song segments on Band 3, Side A. Which type of dance music are they? How are these song selections different?

One example is a Polish polka, characterized by a light quality in the music. It is typically danced with the body weight lifted and the landing precisely controlled (lifted) so that very little sound is made when contacting the floor

The other example is a German polka, characterized by a heavy quality in the music. It is typically danced with stomps, using a flat-footed landing to increase the sounds when contacting the floor.

Success Goal = Identify polkas on the soundsheet (Band 3, Side A) by their contrasting qualities

Your Score =

Song Segment	Type of Polka and Qualities
1	
2	

7. *Name That Dance Music*

a. Again listen to the four song segments on Band 1, Side A. Review your answers to Drill 1 above, then name the kind of social dance music played.

Success Goal = Correctly name the type of dance music for the 4 song segments on Band 1, Side A

Your Score =

Song Segment	Dance Music
1	
2	
3	
4	

b. Now listen to the seven songs presented on Side B of the soundsheet. One of the social dance types is repeated at three different tempos or speeds. For each song, identify the number of beats per measure, the time signature, the count(s) accented, whether the song begins on the downbeat or the upbeat, and the name of the dance music played.

Success Goal = Correctly identify the number of beats per measure, the time signature, the count(s) accented, whether the song begins on the downbeat or the upbeat, and the type of dance music for the 7 songs on Side B

Your Score =

Song Segment	Number of Beats/Measure	Time Signature	Count(s) Accented	Begins on Upbeat	Dance Music
1					
2					
3					
4					
5					
6					
7					

Which dance music is most difficult for you to identify? _____

Which dance music is easiest for you to identify? _____

If you had any difficulties with Drill 7, review the appropriate sections and drills. Your ability to understand musical structure is a foundational skill that you will need to automatically apply as you continue in this book and whenever you dance.

Drill Answers:

Drill 1.   1. Three beats per measure; 3/4 time
           2. Four beats per measure; 4/4 time
           3. Two beats per measure; 2/4 time
           4. Four beats per measure; 4/4 time

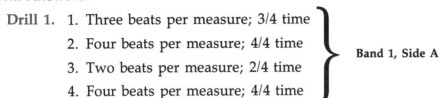

Band 1, Side A

Drill 2.   1. Counts 2, 4
           2. Counts 2, 4
           3. Count 1
           4. Counts 3-and-4
           5. Count 1

Band 2, Side A

Drill 3.   The third segment begins on the upbeat.

Band 1, Side A

Drill 4.   1. Slow
           2. Moderate
           3. Fast

Band 4, Side A

Drill 5.   a. 1. Four beats per measure; 4/4 time; no
              2. Four beats per measure; 4/4 time; no
              3. Three beats per measure; 3/4 time; no
              4. Four beats per measure; 4/4 time; no
              5. Two beats per measure; 2/4 time; yes

           b. 1. Fox-trot
              2. Swing
              3. Waltz
              4. Cha-cha
              5. Polka

Band 2, Side A

Drill 6.   1. Polish polka has light quality to music, with controlled
landings

2. German polka has heavy
quality to music, with forceful, stomp-type landings

Band 3, Side A

Drill 7.   a. 1. Waltz

2. Swing

3. Polka

4. Fox-trot

Band 1, Side A

b. 1. Four beats per measure; 4/4 time;
Counts 2, 4; no; swing (slow tempo)

2. Four beats per measure; 4/4 time;
Counts 3-and-4; no; cha-cha

3. Two beats per measure; 2/4 time;
Count 1; yes; polka

4. Four beats per measure; 4/4 time;
Counts 2, 4; no; fox-trot

5. Four beats per measure; 4/4 time;
Counts 2, 4; no; swing (fast tempo)

6. Three beats per measure; 3/4 time;
Count 1; no; waltz

7. Four beats per measure; 4/4 time;
Counts 2, 4; no; swing (moderate tempo)

Bands 1-7, Side B

Step 3   Connecting Footwork With the Music

A problem unique to social dancing is how to connect your footwork with both the tempo and the beat of the music. This sounds easy, yet it is somewhat more difficult because not only must you step with the beat, but you must also *precisely* time your center of gravity's shift onto the ball of your foot with a specific beat or count. This ear–foot coordination task can be practiced using rhythmical *locomotor movements*, combinations of everyday movements that take you from one place to another. Three locomotor movements are most commonly used in the basic footwork (presented in Steps 4 and 5) for the specific dances covered in this book. Each of these locomotor movements will be described and categorized according to its appropriate rhythm type (even or uneven). The different rhythm types also imply different styling characteristics.

WHY IS IT IMPORTANT TO CONNECT FOOTWORK WITH THE MUSIC?

All dance steps have a foundation in the basic locomotor movements. There are eight basic locomotor movements (the walk, run, leap, jump, hop, gallop, slide, and skip), but only three of them—the walk, hop, and gallop— are most often combined or slightly modified to create "packaged" dance steps.

Whether you want to perform the dance steps that are universally defined or create original dance steps, you need to be able to match specific parts of a locomotor movement with specific counts of the music.

HOW TO CONNECT FOOTWORK WITH EVEN RHYTHMS

An even rhythm reflects a repetitive action that has a steady, soothing quality to it. The walk and the hop each have an even rhythm that can be counted in multiples of 2 or 3. Each whole count of the music corresponds to one

foot action. Thus, consecutive and fluid repetition (an even rhythm) of the walk or hop will have a steady, soothing effect on you. This is part of the appeal and satisfaction of walking and running for exercise.

When you walk in an even rhythm, notice that your foot contacts the floor in a heel-to-toe manner. To connect with the music, time your walking step to let the ball of your foot contact the floor on each whole count of the music. This is not as easy as it sounds, because you incorporate at least five different actions in each walking step—an initial knee bend, an extension of your leg forward from the hip, a heel contact on the floor, a weight shift forward onto the ball of your foot, and a pushoff. In fact, if you watched a film of yourself walking, you would be able to analyze these actions into even more subparts! See the left-hand illustrations in Figure 3.1, a-c, for the Keys to Success for the walk.

Some variation of the walk occurs with all basic dance steps. For example, what changes occur when you walk on each half and whole count of the music? In this variation of the walk, you have to walk twice as fast, forcing you to shorten the length of your step (to a half step), and your body's weight is thrust forward onto the balls of your feet (eliminating the heel contact).

Another variation of the walk that will be used later in the waltz and the fox-trot is a glide step. The glide step is a long, reaching, walk step, also without the heel contact. During the last 2 to 3 inches of the walking step, the ball of the foot slides on the floor. This is a styling change that also helps you avoid stepping on your partner's feet.

To perform a hop in an even rhythm, stand on one leg, and think of Newton's law of action/reaction: For every action there must be an equal and opposite reaction. Thus, bend your standing knee, push off from the ground, rise into the air, then bend that same knee to absorb the force as you land. Four actions (bend, push, rise, and land) must be consecutively repeated so that the timing of the landing occurs on each whole count. With repeated hops, the landing actually becomes the preparation for the next pushoff (see right-hand illustrations in Figure 3.1, a-d). Make sure that your hopping foot begins and lands in the same location—with only upward (and not forward) motion.

When you practice consecutive hopping, be sure to alternate feet after a while to avoid overworking one leg. You will use the hop later in the polka basic step. However, the timing of the hop in the polka basic step will literally be doubled, so that you will land on the upbeat, changing the hop from an even to an uneven rhythm. This timing change modifies the hop to be a skip, which gives it an ''and'' count.

Figure 3.1 Keys to Success:
Even-Rhythm Locomotor Movements

Preparation Phase

Walk

Hop

____ 1. Mentally count to music (whole counts)

____ 2. Identify tempo

____ 3. Prepare to begin moving on upbeat

____

____

____

Execution Phase

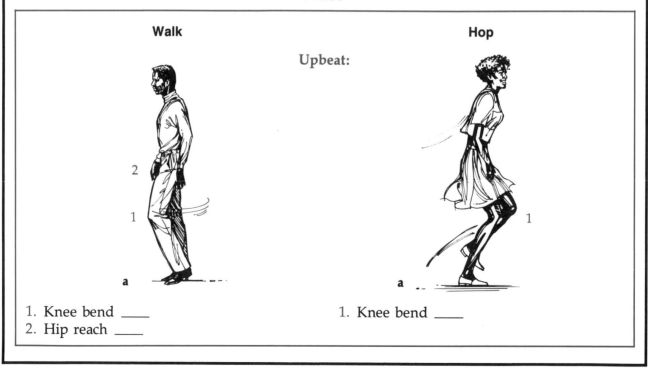

Walk

Hop

Upbeat:

1. Knee bend ____
2. Hip reach ____

1. Knee bend ____

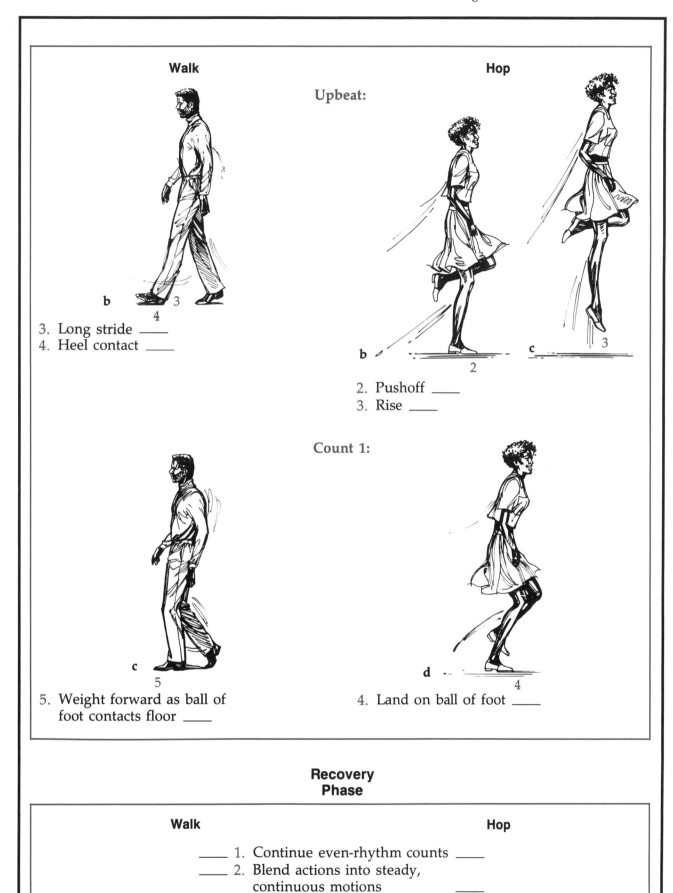

Walk

Hop

Upbeat:

3. Long stride _____
4. Heel contact _____

2. Pushoff _____
3. Rise _____

Count 1:

5. Weight forward as ball of foot contacts floor _____

4. Land on ball of foot _____

Recovery Phase

Walk		Hop
_____ 1.	Continue even-rhythm counts	_____
_____ 2.	Blend actions into steady, continuous motions	_____

HOW TO CONNECT FOOTWORK WITH UNEVEN RHYTHMS

Uneven rhythms reflect the unexpected, which adds variety and interest to dance-step combinations. The gallop has an uneven rhythm because it combines both slow (S) and quick (Q) beats in a recurring pattern.

The gallop alternates a walking step and a leap (transfer of weight from one foot onto the ball of the other foot—like a modified run), with one foot always in the lead. A good image is a horse galloping. A regular walking step is taken on Count 1. During the "and" count, not only is the trailing foot placed slightly behind the lead foot, but both feet also leave the ground prior to landing on only the trailing foot (see the left-hand illustrations in Figure 3.2, a-c).

A popular variation of the gallop in social dance is the triple step. The footwork action is "step, ball, step," which is called a triple step. The timing for the triple step is "1-and-2," or QQS. Use regular walking steps on the whole counts. However, during the "and" count, take a half step and use a pushing action with the ball of your trailing foot. Similarly to the gallop, place the ball of your trailing foot either just beside or slightly behind the heel of your leading foot. However, keep your knees bent slightly during the push with the ball of your trailing foot (Count "and"). This will insure that your head and shoulders remain level (versus rising, as with the gallop). See the right-hand illustrations in Figure 3.2 for the triple step Keys to Success.

The triple step will be referred to often in this book. Also, you may have heard of the "two-step." This is just another name for the triple step, because technically two steps are taken with the same lead foot, and the footwork action is called "step, close, step." There are various styles of two-steps. For example, the country two-step uses a torso lean to the side as the triple step is taken along a diagonal-front path (either right or left). Variations of the triple step are used later in the polka, swing, and cha-cha basic steps.

Figure 3.2 Keys to Success: *Uneven-Rhythm Locomotor Movements*

Preparation Phase

Gallop		Triple Step
____	1. Mentally count to music (whole and half-count combinations)	____
____	2. Identify tempo	____
____	3. Prepare to begin moving on upbeat	____

Execution Phase

Gallop		Triple Step
	Upbeat:	
____	1. Begin step	____
____	2. Heel contact	____

Gallop	Triple Step

Count 1:

a

_____ 3. Transfer weight forward onto ball of foot   _____

Count "and":

b   b

4. Both feet in air prior to landing _____

4. Push with ball of trailing foot (no body lift) _____

Gallop	Triple Step
Count 2:	

_____ 5. Transfer weight onto ball of
same leading foot _____

Recovery Phase

Gallop	Triple Step
1. Momentum (from rising in air) lengthens stride _____	1. Regular walking-step stride _____
_____ 2. Blend actions into fluid motions	_____

Detecting Errors in Connecting Footwork With the Music

The most frequent problems occur when you have to execute a rhythm to musical accompaniment. If you find any of the following timing errors, focus on correcting one at a time. If you are having difficulties that are not on this list, double-check your execution of the basic locomotor movements without any musical accompaniment, but maintain a repetitive rhythm. If necessary, review your understanding of musical structure (see Step 2).

ERROR ⊘	CORRECTION
1. Toe touches floor first during regular walking steps. (Remember that this will not be an error with the gliding variation of the walk for the fox-trot and waltz basics.)	1. Use a normal, heel-to-toe walking step (see Drills 1 and 2 in the next section).
2. Your heel alone contacts the floor on each whole count during forward walking steps.	2. Either speed up your actions or slow down your counts to allow time to smoothly transfer your body weight forward onto the ball of each foot to coincide exactly with each whole count.
3. You travel forward when you hop.	3. Think of ''down, up, down'' actions that are stationary.
4. Either you are late or you add a hop on the ''and'' count within the triple step.	4. Because the triple step's ''and'' count is also a quick beat, it gets only half of a beat. Make sure that you push with the ball of your trailing foot. Keep your knees slightly bent to avoid rising in the air with your head and shoulders (see Drill 8 in the next section).

Connecting Footwork With the Music Drills

1. Establish a Personal Pace

In a large, open space, without music, begin walking in a counterclockwise (CCW) direction. Concentrate on transferring your body weight forward from heel to toe. Establish a comfortable pace that you can easily repeat. Each time you transfer your body weight forward onto the ball of your foot, mentally count in whole numbers (in groups of four or eight counts) to establish a tempo.

Notice the quality of your walking. Is it repetitive, fluid, and even (having one count per step)?

Success Goal = 2 minutes of consecutive, fluid walking (with weight transferred onto the ball of the foot with each whole count)

Your Score = (#) _____ minutes of consecutive, fluid walking, with weight correctly transferred on each whole count

2. *Change Your Personal Pace*

Repeat Drill 1, except alter the tempo and now walk in a clockwise (CW) direction: Thus, if you just walked slowly, now walk at a faster pace, or if you just walked quickly, now slow down your walking pace as you walk in the CW direction. Focus on smoothly connecting your walking steps so that there are no hesitations, and your weight is transferred forward onto the ball of your foot with each whole count. Which personal pace (fast or slow) do you prefer?

Success Goal = 2 minutes of consecutive, fluid walking, with weight correctly transferred on each whole count

Your Score = (#) ____ minutes of consecutive, fluid walking, with weight correctly transferred on each whole count

3. *Walk to a Partner's Pace*

Ask a partner to give you four preparatory claps and then to continuously clap in groups of four counts at a moderate tempo. The first count of each group should be clapped louder so that you can identify the beginning of the measure. Mentally count with your partner's claps. Take one walking step per clap. Make sure that your body weight is transferred forward onto the ball of your foot with each clap.

After 2 minutes of continuous and correctly timed walking to your partner's pace, reverse roles with your partner. You establish a pace for your partner.

Success Goal = 2 minutes of continuous walking to a partner's pace with correct weight transfer on each whole count

Your Score = (#) ____ minutes of continuous walking to a partner's pace with correct weight transfer on each whole count

4. *Walk on Alternate Claps*

Repeat the previous drill, except step on only every other clap. Solve this movement challenge in two different ways:

a. Step on only the odd-numbered claps (Counts 1 and 3); then,
b. Step on only the even-numbered claps (Counts 2 and 4).

Which is easiest for you? Both ways of coordinating your steps to a pace are used later in the packaged dance basics.

After 2 minutes of consecutive and correctly timed walking, switch roles with your partner.

Success Goals = 2 minutes of consecutive and correctly timed walking on only (a) the odd-numbered claps, then (b) the even-numbered claps

Your Score =

a. (#) ____ minutes of consecutive and correctly timed walking (on odd-numbered claps)

b. (#) ____ minutes of consecutive and correctly timed walking (on even-numbered claps)

5. *Evaluate Your Step Length*

The purpose of this drill is to practice the previous two drills together to any 4/4-time music (see Band 4, Side B, of the soundsheet). Alternately take one walking step with each count of the music for the first eight counts, then take one walking step on only the even-numbered counts for the next eight counts. Thus, the footwork actions alternate eight walks, then four walks, but the total number of counts is 16.

Consecutively repeat this two-part combination for the length of one song (in 4/4 time). Notice what length of step you take for both parts. In which part do you have the shorter strides?

Reverse roles with your partner, and give each other feedback on the actual lengths of your walking steps. There should be an obvious step-length difference: first short, then long.

Success Goals = Correctly identify your stride lengths when stepping (a) on each count, then (b) only on even-numbered counts

Your Score =

a. _____ The length of your stride when stepping on each count (short or long)

b. _____ The length of your stride when stepping only on the even-numbered counts (short or long)

6. *Walking Sequence Using Forward and Backward Directions*

The purpose of this drill is to vary the direction you move in while walking, to create a sequence that can be repeated for the length of one song (in 4/4 time). Face one wall to establish a "front." Using your right foot to start, take four walking steps forward, then four walking steps backward. Keep repeating this pattern.

Slowly add a rocking motion when you change directions, so that you make a smooth transition between moving forward and backward. To do this, bend your knees more on both the fourth count forward and the first count backward, and keep your feet in a forward-backward stride position. Smoothly repeat for at least 2 consecutive minutes to any 4/4-time music.

Then repeat this walking sequence, starting with your left foot. Again, make the transitions between the direction changes as smoothly as possible and correctly timed with the music.

Success Goals = 2 minutes of continuous repetition of the walking sequence with smooth transitions, to music, starting with (a) the right foot, then (b) the left foot

Your Score =

a. (#) ____ minutes of continuous repetition with smooth transitions (starting with the right foot)

b. (#) ____ minutes of continuous repetition with smooth transitions (starting with the left foot)

7. Schottische Sequence

By combining three walking steps and a hop within four counts, you have a well-known folk-dance step, the schottische. It is included here to give you additional practice with even rhythms that combine two different locomotor steps. Later, the schottische will be used to help you create your own social dance (in Step 12).

Without music, practice the schottische in place. Then, starting with your right foot first, do one schottische while moving in each of the following directions:

a. Forward, backward; repeat
b. Right, left; repeat
c. Turning 360 degrees CW, then CCW; repeat

Now you are ready to put all three parts together into a continuous schottische sequence. Repeat the entire schottische sequence at least four times without getting off-count.

With music, repeat the schottische sequence to any 4/4-time music (see Band 7, Side B, of the soundsheet). Make sure that your schottische sequences are both continuous and correctly timed with the music.

Success Goals = 4 continuous schottische sequences correctly timed (a) with the counts, then (b) with the music

Your Score =

a. (#) ____ continuous schottische sequences (timed with the counts)

b. (#) ____ continuous schottische sequences (timed with the music)

8. Triple Step

How can you take six steps within four counts? If you get stuck, try adding a half step on the "and" between the whole counts, but not on the upbeat.

One solution is to group three steps together, and do two consecutive triple steps alternating your lead foot for each triple step (see the right-hand illustrations in Figure 3.2). Remember that the middle step gets a half beat, as does the first step, and it trails the lead foot. Do a "step, ball, step" (triple step) for at least eight measures of any 4/4-time music (see Band 1, Side B, of the soundsheet).

Success Goal = 16 consecutive triple steps without getting off-count with the music

Your Score = (#) ____ consecutive triple steps without getting off-count with the music

9. Triple-Step Sequence

The purpose of this drill is to show how repetition can give you more time to prepare for a direction change.

    a. Face one wall. Take four triple steps forward, then four triple steps backward. Check that your middle step is taken with your weight on the ball of your foot and that its placement is either behind the heel of the lead foot when going forward or close to the toe of the lead foot when going backward. You will not have enough time to place your heel down on the ''and'' steps. Thus, continuously repeat the following triple-step sequence to any 4/4-time music (see Band 1, Side B, of the soundsheet), starting with your right foot.

Number of Triple Steps	Direction	Counts
4	forward	1-and-2, 3-and-4, 5-and-6, 7-and-8
4	backward	1-and-2, 3-and-4, 5-and-6, 7-and-8

    b. Now, repeat the triple-step sequence (in part a), except do only two triple steps forward, then two backward. Notice that you now have less time to make your direction changes.

Success Goals = 2 minutes of continous repetition of the triple-step sequence, to music, using (a) 4 triple steps forward, then backward; then (b) 2 triple steps forward, then backward

Your Score =

    a. (#) ____ minutes of continuous repetition of the triple-step sequence (using 4 triple steps) to music

    b. (#) ____ minutes of continuous repetition of the triple-step sequence (using 2 triple steps) to music

10. Combined Sequence of Even and Uneven Rhythms

The following sequence combines even and uneven rhythms by alternating two locomotor movements (the walk and triple step) and two directions (forward and backward):

    a. Four walking steps forward; four walking steps backward; repeat
    b. Four triple steps forward; four triple steps backward; repeat

Starting with your right foot, do this combined even- and uneven-rhythm sequence continuously to any 4/4-time music (see Band 2, Side B). Make sure that your transitions between the different locomotor movements and the different directions are smoothly executed and correctly timed with the music.

Success Goal = 2 minutes of continuous repetition of the combined even- and uneven-rhythm sequence to music, fluidly

Your Score =   (#) _____ minutes of continuous repetition of the combined even- and uneven-rhythm sequence to music, fluidly

Connecting Footwork With the Music
Keys to Success Checklists

It is critical that you be able to match your footwork with both the beat and the tempo of the music. Ask a trained partner or your teacher to use the checklists in Figures 3.1 and 3.2 to evaluate your ability to properly execute both even- and uneven-rhythm locomotor movements without getting off-count with the music. Especially be sure that you are properly executing the walk, hop, and the triple step to music. Use the gallop checklist more for identifying potential errors that may flaw your execution of the triple step, which will be used throughout the rest of this book.

Step 4 **Uneven-Rhythm Dance Basics**

Steps 4 and 5 show you how to do the packaged basic dance steps that are traditionally associated with ballroom or social dance. This means that you will be able to attend ballroom dances almost anywhere and recognize these basic steps and their corresponding music. The five basic dance steps that use uneven rhythms are the triple lindy (swing), cha-cha, polka, magic step (fox-trot), and single lindy (swing). Each of these five basic steps connects one or more locomotor movements with the music. At this point, the basics are to be practiced with a partner, but without touching. This delay gives you time to make your movements automatic before you have to worry about leading or following or working in unison with someone else.

There are only two strategies that you need to use when you learn how to combine the various locomotor movements to fit uneven rhythms: (a) Combine two locomotor movements, or (b) alter the timing by incorporating a hold or pause. The music's tempo (slow, medium, or fast) determines the order in which the uneven-rhythm dance basics are presented. It is important to become aware of tempo, because certain tempos lend themselves to only a particular basic dance step, whereas other tempos give you the choice of which basic dance step to execute. Eventually, you will need to decide which basic dance step best fits the music. For example, when polka music begins, it is very obvious that a polka step is appropriate. However, when swing music is played, you must identify the tempo to select which basic swing step (out of three) best fits the music. Still other situations are not so eas-

ily determined. It is not uncommon to see dancers performing either fox-trot or swing basic steps to fast fox-trot music. The drill sections in Steps 4 and 5 will help you practice some of this decision making.

Two observable differences among the basic steps to be aware of are in the location and the direction of the flow of traffic. For example, the fox-trot, waltz, and polka basic steps are typically performed in a CCW direction around the perimeter of the floor, which is called the "line of direction" (LOD). Yet, the swing and cha-cha basic steps are performed within a much smaller space, or "spot" on the dance floor.

WHY ARE THE UNEVEN-RHYTHM DANCE BASICS IMPORTANT?

The uneven-rhythm dance basics represent some of the most popular social dances, and they are fun to do because they lend variety to your evening. Typically, an evening of songs includes the highest percent of fox-trot and waltz, while the swing, cha-cha, and polka represent the third, fourth, and fifth highest percent of all songs played.

Even though the basic steps may be similarly derived, each dance has its own styling characteristics. These styles should be recognizably different. Your challenge is to not only understand the strategies behind how to create the basic steps, but also to perform each dance with the appropriate styling to reflect its uniqueness. It is not enough to execute the basic steps well; you must also add the unique "flavor" or "character" of each of the dances.

Strategy 1: Combine Two Locomotor Movements

By using Strategy 1, you can learn three basic steps: the triple lindy (swing), the cha-cha, and the polka. The first two are very similar, as both combine walks and the triple step. However, the order of these two locomotor movements is reversed. The triple lindy combines two triple steps and two modified walks, whereas the cha-cha combines two modified walks and a modified triple step. The polka basic step combines a hop and a triple step.

TRIPLE-LINDY BASIC (SWING)

The swing, which evolved from the jazz era of the 1920s, was first known as the jitterbug. Later, this American dance was called the "lindy hop" in honor of Charles Lindberg, who flew solo across the Atlantic in 1927. In time, the lindy hop became known simply as the lindy. Because of the popularity of swing bands during the 1930s and 1940s, the lindy was called the swing. This name has held throughout the rock-and-roll (the 1950s and 1960s) and the new-wave eras (to the present).

The swing is fun to do because of its styling freedom (erect posture is not as important in the swing). It is characterized by torso leans and a jazzy, syncopated style. The swing is a spot dance—each couple stakes out a small section of the dance floor. The many variations of the swing allow partners to rotate around each other within a circle approximately 10 feet in diameter.

There are three types of swing steps—triple lindy, double lindy, and single lindy—depending on the tempo of the music: slow, moderate, or fast, respectively. The triple lindy utilizes triple steps, as its name implies, to slow, syncopated music. The double-lindy footwork fits an even rhythm, so it is covered in Step 5. The single lindy is used for very fast swing music, and also uses a different footwork strategy, so it is covered under Strategy 2.

The entire triple lindy takes six counts, which are repeated throughout a song. These counts can be called out according to each step's rhythmic count, duration, and direction, as follows:

Total Counts: Six (accents on even Counts 2, 4, and 6)

Rhythmic Counts: 1-and-2; 3-and-4; 5, 6

Duration of Steps: Quick-quick-slow; quick-quick-slow; slow, slow

Direction of Steps: Triple step forward; triple step backward; ball-change (in place)

To execute the triple lindy, stand in correct body alignment facing forward. Either set up with a partner or imagine a partner standing beside you, with the man on the left and the woman on the right. Angle your feet and body to stand on a 45-degree angle toward your partner (Figure 4.1a). Move your body weight to the balls of your feet. Listen for the tempo (it should be slow). Mentally count in fours to the established tempo and prepare to step on any first count with your outside foot (the foot farthest away from your partner).

To add styling, slightly drop your outside shoulder and let your torso lean as you take your triple step forward with your outside

Triple Lindy									
Footwork actions	step-ball-step			step-ball-step			ball	change	
Rhythmic counts	1	&	2	3	&	4	5	6	
Total counts	1		2	3		4	5	6	
4/4 time signature	1		2	3		4	1	2	3	4
			>			>		>		>

foot, keeping most of your body weight on the balls of your feet (Counts 1-and-2). Then reverse your torso lean by dropping your inside shoulder (the shoulder closest to your partner) just before taking a triple step backward with your inside foot, keeping your weight on the balls of your feet (Counts 3-and-4).

For styling within Counts 5 and 6, align your body so that your hips, shoulders, and head are centered over your feet. Keep your body weight on your inside foot. Bring the ball of your outside foot approximately 2 inches be-

hind the heel of your inside foot (fifth position, in ballet terms). As you step on the ball of your outside foot, simultaneously bend your inside knee and slightly lift the inside foot not more than a few inches off the floor (Count 5). Then step down on the inside foot without changing its original position (Count 6). Remember to keep your upper body erect during Counts 5 and 6. The footwork actions for Counts 5 and 6 can be summarized simply: ball-change.

Figure 4.1 illustrates the triple-lindy execution Keys to Success, which involve eight actual steps taken to six counts of the music.

Figure 4.1 Keys to Success: Triple-Lindy Basic (Slow Swing Tempo)

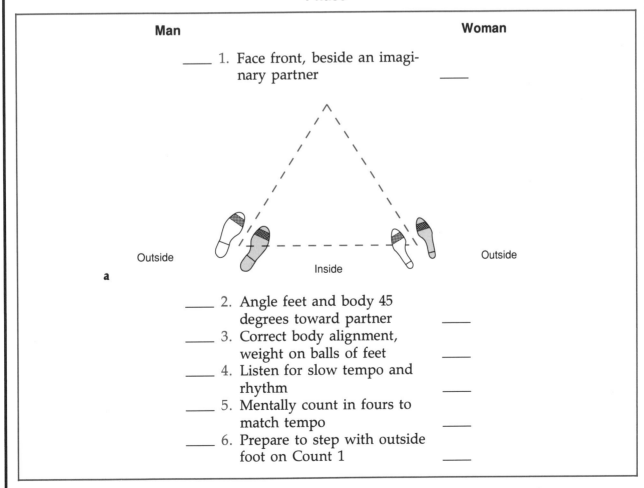

Preparation Phase

Man   **Woman**

_____ 1. Face front, beside an imaginary partner   _____

Outside   Inside   Outside

a

_____ 2. Angle feet and body 45 degrees toward partner   _____

_____ 3. Correct body alignment, weight on balls of feet   _____

_____ 4. Listen for slow tempo and rhythm   _____

_____ 5. Mentally count in fours to match tempo   _____

_____ 6. Prepare to step with outside foot on Count 1   _____

Execution Phase

Man	Woman

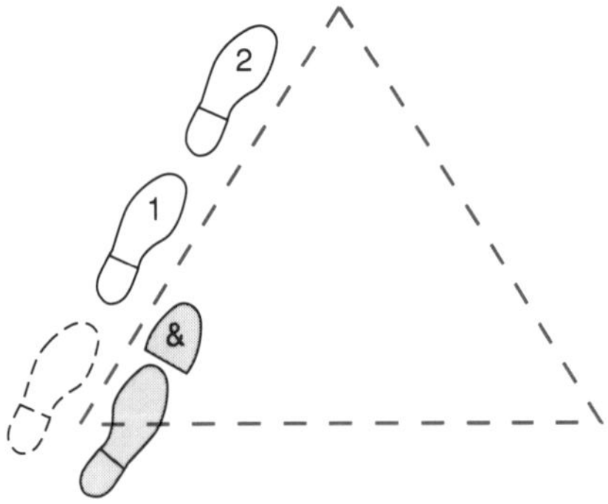

Man

b

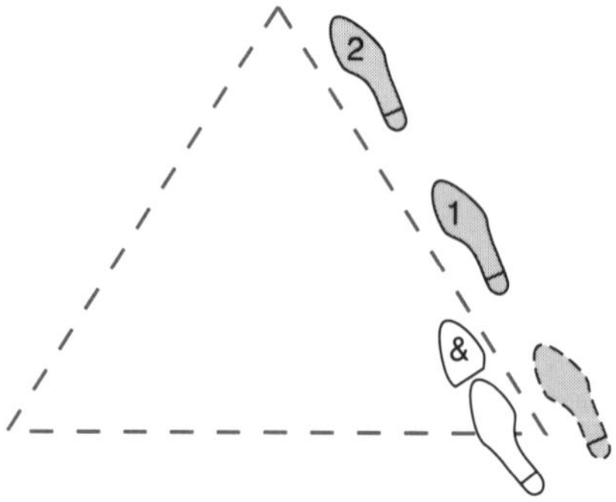

Woman

b

1. **Counts 1-and-2**:
   ____ Drop outside shoulder ____
   ____ Let torso lean ____
   ____ Triple step forward ____

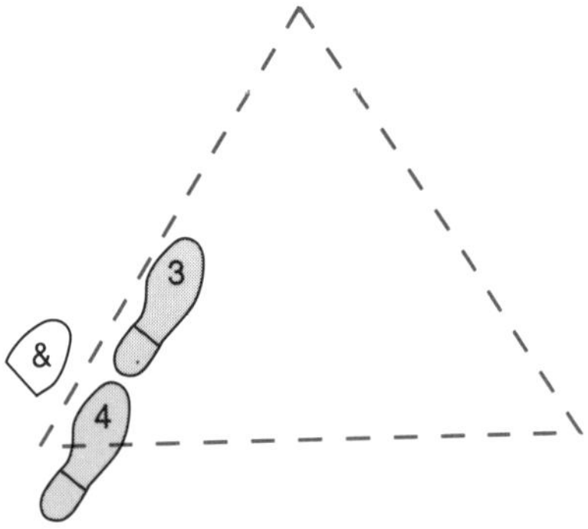

c

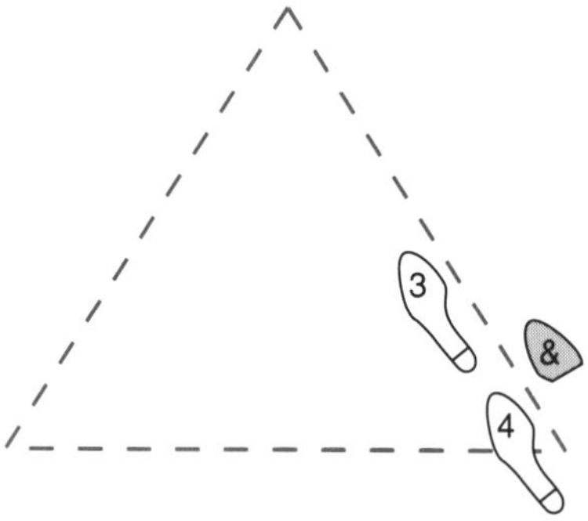

c

2. **Counts 3-and-4**:
   ____ Drop inside shoulder ____
   ____ Let torso lean ____
   ____ Triple step backward ____

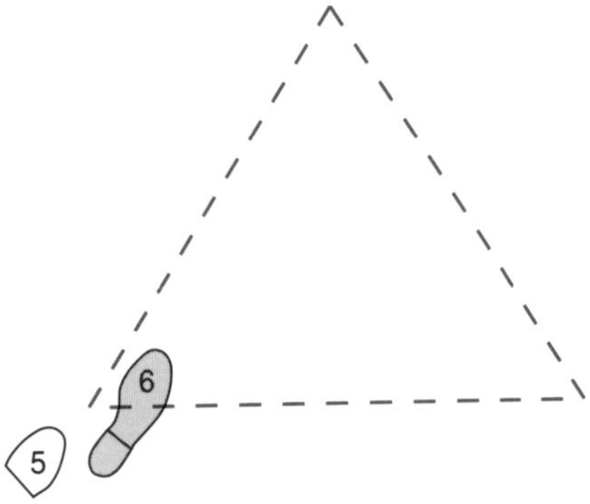

d

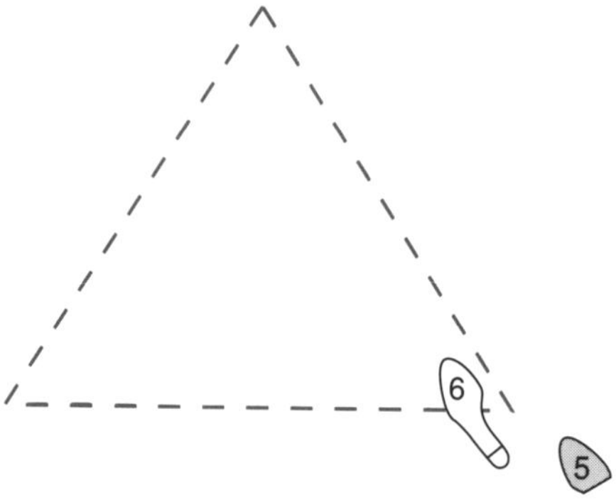

d

3. **Count 5**:
   ____ Ball (step on ball of outside
   foot, 2 inches behind heel of
   inside foot, as you lift inside
   knee and foot) ____

Man	Woman
4. **Count 6**: ____ Change (step down on inside foot without changing its location) ____	

Styling Phase

Man	Woman
____ 1. Maintain consecutive six- count rhythm ____	
____ 2. Stay within your spot ____	
3. Add jazzy, syncopated styling:	
____ • Drop shoulder with both triple steps ____	
____ • Keep upright posture on Counts 5 and 6 ____	
____ • Let your knees bend slightly ____	
____ • Crisply execute steps ____	
____ • Keep motions fluid ____	

Detecting Triple-Lindy Errors

There are two common errors to look for when executing the triple-lindy basic step. If you have these problems, focus on correcting only one at a time.

ERROR 🚫

CORRECTION

1. Your body lifts in the air on the "and" counts within the triple steps.	1. Make sure that you control your small, quick "and" steps by bending your knees and keeping your head height level (rather than rising, as you did in the gallop).

ERROR   **CORRECTION**

2. You step so far back with your outside foot during your ball-change that your upper torso sways back, then forward.

2. Place your ball step up to one half of a step behind your inside foot's heel. This keeps your posture more erect, without the upper torso lean you would have away from your partner if you used a full step. Also, the music's speed does not give you enough time to take a large step back.

Drills for the Triple-Lindy Basic (Swing)

1. Execution Challenge

Experiment with the following questions: How would you do one triple step forward and one triple step backward? Can you take small steps? Can you let one foot lead forward and the opposite foot lead backward? Can you add two small steps, one backward, then one forward? What happens when you start with a different foot first?

To answer these questions, follow the Keys to Success in Figure 4.1 for the triple-lindy basic.

Repeat the entire six-count triple-lindy basic step without music. Mentally count the rhythmic counts, and make sure that you are stepping on each count: "1-and-2, 3-and-4, 5, 6."

Then repeat the triple-lindy basic to slow swing music, making sure that you add your torso leans only on the triple steps forward and backward. Continue to practice the triple-lindy basic to slow swing music until you can move almost without thinking about your footwork for the length of one song.

Success Goals =

   a. 8 repetitions of the triple-lindy basic with proper styling (without music)

   b. Continuous repetition of the triple-lindy basic with proper styling for the length of 1 slow swing song

Your Score =

   a. (#) ____ repetitions of the triple-lindy basic with proper styling (without music)

   b. ____ Continuous repetition of the triple-lindy basic with proper styling for the length of 1 slow swing song (yes or no)

2. Starting and Stopping With the Music

Set up as in the previous drill. Ask a third person to play Band 1, Side B, on the soundsheet. Mentally count in fours to get the tempo. Because you are not touching your partner yet, you'll need to let your partner (and yourself) know when to begin with the music. So, on any Count 1, verbally say "1, 2, ready, begin." Then execute the triple-lindy basic with proper styling, moving in unison with your partner (like a mirror image), at least six times before stopping. Alternately, continue to start and stop for the length of the song. As you practice more, you'll soon be able to signal your partner nonverbally by your outside shoulder drop and torso leans. As you are working with a partner, make sure that you both get a chance to verbally start the other.

Success Goal = 6 consecutive repetitions of the triple-lindy basic with proper styling, and with at least 6 stops and restarts to slow swing music

Your Score = (#) ____ repetitions of the triple-lindy basic with proper styling, and with (#) ____ stops and restarts to music

3. Footwork for Half Turns

It is not necessary to practice the following turns with a partner at this point. All of the turns are executed on Count 2. Starting with your outside foot (the man's left, the woman's right), take one triple step forward and freeze on Count 2. Repeat, and check that your body weight is transferred onto the ball of your outside foot.

From your freeze position, gather your momentum and spin your body 360 degrees (or more) either CW or CCW. If you can spin at least one full turn, then a half turn (which is what is desired) will be very easy for you. If you turned CW, now turn CCW (or vice versa). You'll need to be able to spin on the ball of your outside foot equally smoothly in either direction.

Without music, do a half turn CW on Count 2 of your triple step forward, and continue with your triple step backward, and ball-change.

Again, without music, repeat your triple-lindy basic with a half turn CCW. Double-check that your spin occurs on Count 2.

Then continuously repeat the triple-lindy basic with CW and CCW half turns (in random order) to slow swing music. Continue practicing until you feel comfortable turning in either half-turn direction.

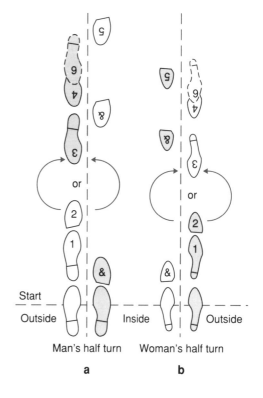

Man's half turn   Woman's half turn

a   b

Success Goals =

a. 4 consecutive triple-lindy basics with a CW half turn on Count 2 (without music)

b. 4 consecutive triple-lindy basics with a CCW half turn on Count 2 (without music)

c. 8 consecutive triple-lindy basics with CW and CCW half turns (in random order) on Count 2 to slow swing music

Your Score =

a. (#) ___ consecutive triple-lindy basics CW (without music)

b. (#) ___ consecutive triple-lindy basics CCW (without music)

c. (#) ___ consecutive triple-lindy basics CW and CCW (with music)

CHA-CHA BASIC

The most popular Latin dance is the cha-cha, which was originally called the cha-cha-cha in Cuba during the mid-1950s—to reflect the three quick steps used in the footwork and the calypso sounds heard in the music. Finding the three ''chas'' cumbersome, however, Americans shortened the name.

The cha-cha is a blend of other dances. It has a rhythm similar to the mambo, a triple step as well as many step variations like the triple lindy, and styling similar to that of the rhumba. Due to the Latin influence, the cha-cha is smooth and flirtatious—for instance, you look at your partner out of the corners of your eyes as you tilt your head slightly to tease and challenge your partner to follow or look at you. Another uniqueness of the cha-cha is ''talking'' with your hands. You can ''talk'' with your hands by keeping your elbows bent 90 degrees and fairly close to your sides, but allowing your forearms and hands to move as you move: both rotating the wrists and letting the arms move forward and backward from the shoulders. Another way to give the illusion of a challenge is to follow your partner's forward and backward movements—alternately, one advances and the other retreats. Thus, you seem to be connected, but you are actually approximately 2 feet apart and facing each other (in a position called the ''shine'' position).

Following the Latin influence, it is typical to start moving on the second count. However, this timing variation is difficult for beginners, so only the version starting on the first count is described. Also, you may perform the cha-cha either with a rocking motion (American version) or with Cuban motion (the Latin version). Again, the American version is described because it is the easiest and fastest to learn. Later, when you feel very comfortable with the American cha-cha, you can consider modifying your cha-cha to include Cuban motion, which will not be covered in detail here. Briefly, however, Cuban motion results from alternately bending one knee as you straighten the other—the hips only appear to do all the work!

The cha-cha basic includes two parts: a forward half and a back half, with each half taking four counts. These counts may be called out in the following ways:

Total Counts: Eight

Rhythmic Counts: 1, 2, 3-and-4; 1, 2, 3-and-4; or 1, 2, 3-and-4; 5, 6, 7-and-8

Duration of Steps: Slow, slow, quick-quick-slow (both halves)

Length of Steps: Long, long, short-short-short (both halves)

Direction of Steps:

- The man starts with the forward half—forward, back, back-back-back
- The woman starts with the backward half—back, forward, forward-forward-forward

Cha-Cha	Forward half					Backward half				
Footwork actions	fwd	bwd	bwd-bwd-bwd			bwd	fwd	fwd-fwd-fwd		
Rhythmic counts	1 >	2 >	3 >	& >	4 >	1 >	2 >	3 >	& >	4 >
Total counts	1	2	3		4	5	6	7		8
4/4 time signature	1	2	3		4	1	2	3		4

Setup: Start in the shine position facing your partner, approximately 2 feet apart without touching. Bend your elbows 90 degrees, hold elbows in close to the sides of the body, and face palms of hands down. The shine position allows your hands to be free to "talk" to your partner (as described previously). Keep your shoulders and upper torso still and erect, letting the lower body action result from using either a rocking motion (American version) or Cuban motion. With both versions, keep your entire foot flat to the floor by bending your foot approximately 90 degrees at the ankle throughout.

The man starts the forward half with his left foot; the woman simultaneously starts the backward half with her right foot.

Counts 1, 2: The man steps forward and the woman steps backward on Count 1. Keep your feet in a stride position (with one foot approximately 12 to 18 inches in front of the other). Use a rocking motion to smoothly change direction (the man rocks back onto his right foot, the woman rocks forward onto her left foot) on Count 2.

Counts 3-and-4: To modify the original triple step to fit this cha-cha-cha rhythm, you need to give equal length to each part of your triple step (the middle "and" *should not* be placed behind as was previously done in the triple lindy). Imagine that the three triple steps are three small running steps. Let the stepping foot lead (alternating left and right foot) as you travel, and advance each foot approximately half the length of your own foot (whether traveling forward or backward). Do not let only one foot lead as you did in the triple-lindy basic. Keep both knees slightly bent and your head level as you travel either backward or forward.

Notice that in the "forward half" of the cha-cha basic, only the first step is forward; the remaining steps (Counts 2, 3-and-4) are taken while moving backward. The footwork actions are L, R, L-R-L.

In the "backward half" of the cha-cha basic, only the first step is backward; all other steps (Counts 2, 3-and-4) are taken while moving forward. The footwork actions are R, L, R-L-R.

See Figure 4.2 for a summary of how to execute both halves of the American version of the cha-cha.

Figure 4.2 Keys to Success:
   Cha-Cha Basic

**Preparation
Phase**

1. Face partner, without touching (shine position) ____
2. Feet parallel and 2 inches apart ____
3. Weight on balls of feet ____
4. Knees slightly flexed and relaxed ____
5. Elbows bent 90 degrees, palms facing down ____
6. Listen for tempo ____
7. Mentally count rhythm ____
8. Prepare to step on Count 1 (flex foot at ankle) ____

a

**Execution
Phase**

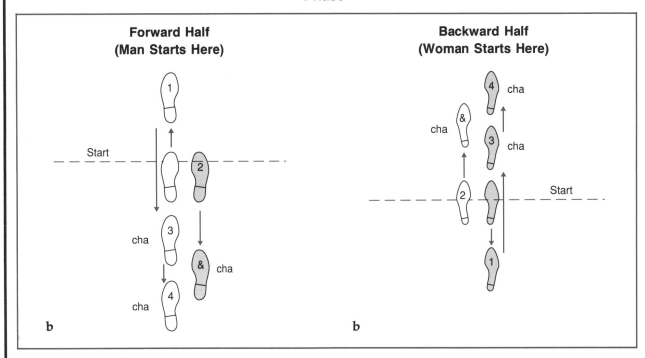

**Forward Half
(Man Starts Here)**

Start

1
2
cha 3
& cha
cha 4

b

**Backward Half
(Woman Starts Here)**

4 cha
cha &
3 cha
2   Start
1

b

Forward Half
(Man Starts Here)

1. **Count 1**:
   Left foot steps
   forward ____
   Keep right foot in original position ____
2. **Count 2**:
   Rock weight back onto
   right foot ____
   Keep left foot in same
   position ____
   Prepare to move
   backward ____
3. **Counts 3-and-4**:
   Modified triple step
   backward (advance one
   half length of own foot
   on each step, L-R-
   L) ____
   Keep both knees
   slightly bent ____

Backward Half
(Woman Starts Here)

1. **Count 1**:
   Right foot steps
   backward ____
   Keep left foot in
   original position ____
2. **Count 2**:
   Rock weight forward
   onto left foot ____
   Keep right foot in
   same position ____
   Prepare to move
   forward ____
3. **Counts 3-and-4**:
   Modified triple step (advance one half length of
   own foot on each step
   forward, R-L-R) ____
   Keep both knees
   slightly bent ____

Styling
Phase

1. Follow partner's forward
   and backward
   movements ____
2. Maintain consecutive,
   fluid rhythm and
   tempo ____
3. Keep head level
   throughout (relax
   knees) ____
4. Let hands "talk" as you
   move:

   • Elbows in close to
     body ____

   • Palms held down ____
   • Wrists rotate
     freely ____
   • Arms move freely
     from the shoulder in
     forward/backward
     directions ____

5. Look through corners of
   eyes at partner ____

Drills for the Cha-Cha Basic

1. Execution Challenge

Experiment with the following questions: How can you connect one rock step (from Step 3, Drill 6) and one triple step (from Step 3, Drill 8)? How can you repeat this connection to move both forward and backward? With only one repetition of each action, notice how quickly you have to execute both of your movements and make your decisions as to which direction to move in.

To answer the previous questions, follow the Keys to Success in Figure 4.2 for the cha-cha basic.

Repeat both halves of the cha-cha basic as you face your partner (in shine position). Count the rhythmic counts (1, 2, 3-and-4) out loud to a self-paced tempo that works best for you and your partner.

Success Goal = 8 consecutive repetitions of the cha-cha basic in shine position to the tempo of your self-paced counts

Your Score = (#) _____ consecutive repetitions of the cha-cha basic to self-paced counts

2. Adjusting to the Music

Repeat Drill 1 to slow cha-cha music (use Band 2, Side B, of the soundsheet). At first, it may seem difficult to find music that is slow enough; if the music's tempo is too fast for you and your partner, practice to a self-paced count slightly faster than your pace in the previous drill. Then, when you are ready, practice to the music.

Success Goal = 16 consecutive repetitions of the cha-cha basic in shine position to slow music

Your Score = (#) _____ consecutive repetitions of the cha-cha basic in shine position to slow music

3. Adding Styling

You have already begun to add styling by following your partner's footwork actions and direction changes. The purpose of this drill is to refine your styling even more. In the shine position, imagine that you have horizontal strings connecting the two of you at your shoulders, hips, and ankles. As one moves either forward or backward, the other automatically follows in unison. This invisible connection with your partner helps you to move fluidly with your partner and also presents you both with the challenge of following the other's directional changes. Repeat the cha-cha basic at least 16 times with your partner to music, and check yourself on the following cha-cha styling points:

- Hold elbows at 90-degree angles.
- Keep palms down.
- Let wrists and forearms rotate freely—"talking" to your partner!

Success Goal = 16 consecutive repetitions of the cha-cha basic in shine position to music and following a partner

Your Score = (#) _____ consecutive repetitions of the cha-cha basic in shine position to music and following a partner

POLKA BASIC

The polka basic step originated as a folk-dance step found in English country dances, German folk dances, and Polish folk dances. However, the styling of each varies—from a light, springy quality to a heavy, forceful quality. The polka uses the versatile triple step and adds a modified hop on the upbeat. At first the polka may seem very difficult, because not only must you make more actions than with any other basic step, but you must also do them very quickly. Because the polka is so vigorous, you will need to build up your stamina to last the entire length of a song (and ultimately an evening's worth of polkas and other dances!).

The polka step uses two counts, or one measure of 2/4-time music. However, you need to repeat the polka step on both sides, so there is a total of four counts. These counts may be called out in the following ways:

Total Counts: Four (accents on Counts 1 and 3

Rhythmic Counts: And-1-and-2, and-1-and-2; or and-1-and-2-and-3-and-4

Duration of Steps: Quick, slow, quick, slow (both sides start on the upbeat)

Direction of Steps: In place, forward, close, forward (both sides)

To set up for the polka at this point, stand beside a partner (with the man on the left and the woman on the right) without touching hands. Transfer your body weight onto your inside foot.

The polka basic footwork actions are "hop, step, ball, step." These four footwork actions combine the modified hop with the triple step and coincide with the rhythmic counts "and-1-and-2." As you repeat the polka basic on both sides, the hop actually blends with the end of the triple step to modify the hop to be an uneven rhythm (giving it a half count like a skip). If it is too difficult for you to do this modified hop on the upbeat, you may want to start with the triple step on the downbeat, and then add the modified hop on the "and" count prior to your next triple step (the upbeat). These actions become continuous movements with no obvious starting or stopping points.

Polka		One side				Other side			
Footwork actions	hop	step-close-step			hop	step-close-step			hop
Rhythmic counts	_&_	_1_	_&_	_2_	_&_	_3_	_&_	_4_	_&_
Total counts		_1_		_2_		_3_		_4_	
2/4 time signature		_1_		_2_		_1_		_2_	
		>				>			

The polka basic step alternates fast and slow actions. Each "and" receives one half-count, which only gives you time to place the ball of your foot on the floor. Thus, both your "and" counts are executed quickly with almost no traveling forward. Figure 4.3 shows the Keys to Success for the polka basic step.

Figure 4.3 Keys to Success: Polka Basic

Preparation Phase

1. Stand beside partner (man left, woman right) ____
2. Body erect ____
3. Weight on inside foot ____

4. Listen for tempo ____
5. Mentally count "and-1-and-2" ____
6. Prepare to hop on the upbeat ____

Execution Phase

1. **Count "and"**: Hop on inside foot ____
2. **Counts 1-and-2**: Triple step ____
3. **Repeat on opposite side** ____

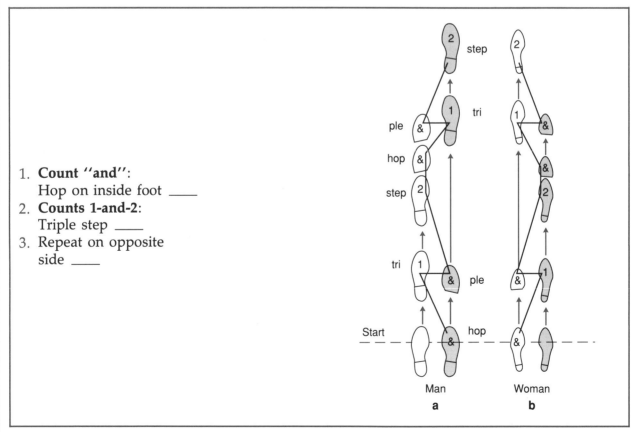

**Styling
Phase**

1. Consecutively alternate footwork to rhythm ____
2. Vertical motion *only* on upbeat ____
3. Forward motion *only* on the triple step ____
4. Use small steps ____

5. Gradually increase tempo to move with the music ____
6. If you "lose it," smile, and start again ____
7. Build up stamina to last an entire song—you can do it ____

Drills for the Polka Basic

1. Execution Challenge

Because you combine two different locomotor movements in the polka basic step, it is helpful to practice each separately, then to put them together.

a. As previously mentioned, the last step of the triple step should blend into the hop (on the upbeat of the music). To practice blending these actions, repeat only two actions—a step and a hop—commonly called a skip. Think back to your carefree childhood days when you used to skip. Without any music, practice skipping down the length of the room. Notice that your skip alternately combines a step and a hop.

What rhythm are you using, even or uneven?

Turn around, skip back to your starting position, and check that you are doing an uneven, "1-and" rhythm (either verbally or silently) as you simultaneously step and hop. Each whole count should coincide with a step, and each half count should coincide with a partial foot contact with the floor (the ball of the foot only).

Again, skip down and back the length of the room. This time, also experiment with bringing your free foot and ankle forward to prepare for the next skip, rather than letting your foot and ankle trail behind you. If you leave your foot and ankle behind you during the "and" count, you will be late with the rhythm.

b. Practice the triple step as you travel down and back the length of the room. This repeats an earlier drill (Step 3, Drill 8).

Is your triple-step rhythm even or uneven? Make sure that you can do an uneven rhythm, "1-and-2," repetitively. Each foot alternately should lead twice (on each whole count). The "and" step should be taken on the ball of your foot, directly behind the heel of the leading foot.

c. Without music, combine the hop (part a) and the triple step (part b) to do consecutive polka basic steps in a large circle around the room. Make sure that you are blending all parts into one continuous motion. If you need to, review the polka basic Keys to Success in Figure 4.3.

Success Goals =

a. 16 correctly executed skips without music

b. 16 correctly executed triple steps without music

c. 16 correctly executed polka basic steps without music

Your Score =

a. (#) _____ correctly executed skips

b. (#) _____ correctly executed triple steps

c. (#) _____ correctly executed polka basic steps

2. Move to the Music

a. Moving down and back the length of the room, repeat the polka basic steps to very slow polka music (use Band 3, Side B, of the soundsheet), while you either verbally or silently count the appropriate uneven-rhythm pattern. Ask your partner to check that you correctly time your footwork actions with the music. If the music is too fast, repeat part c of the previous drill until you can blend your actions to fit the music.

b. Repeat your polka basic steps while moving CCW in a large circle around the perimeter of the room (in LOD). As before, travel down the length of the room. However, once you get to the end of the room, think of moving on a curved line, such that you rotate CCW ever so slightly each time you repeat a polka basic step. Then travel the length of the room again, and travel on a curved line when you get to the opposite end of the room. The advantage of moving CCW is that you start and stop less often.

Success Goals =

a. 16 correctly executed polka basics to music, traveling the length of the room and back

b. 32 correctly executed polka basics to music, traveling in LOD

Your Score =

a. (#) _____ correctly executed polka basics to music, traveling the length of the room and back

b. (#) _____ correctly executed polka basics to music, traveling in LOD

3. Polka Basic in Three Directions

The purpose of this drill is to correctly execute the polka basic step in three different ways: (a) moving either CW or CCW within a small circle, (b) repeating a short sequence, and (c) starting the sequence with either foot.

As you practice this drill to music, first travel down the length of the room and back. Once you know the following sequence very well, repeat it while traveling in the LOD:

- Four polka basic steps forward
- Four polka basic steps moving CW in a small semicircle
- Four polka basic steps forward
- Four polka basic steps moving CCW in a small semicircle

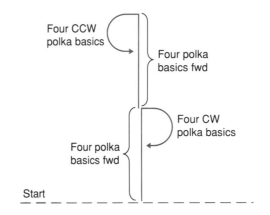

Do this sequence eight times, starting with your right foot. Then repeat it eight times, starting with your left foot.

Which starting foot is easiest for you? (Later, when a partner is added, women will start with the right foot, and men will start with the left foot.)

Success Goals =

  a. 8 consecutive repetitions of the polka sequence to music, starting with the right foot

  b. 8 consecutive repetitions of the polka sequence to music, starting with the left foot

Your Score =

  a. (#) _____ consecutive repetitions of the sequence, starting with the right foot

  b. (#) _____ consecutive repetitions of the sequence, starting with the left foot

4. Connecting Arms and Feet

This drill has three parts: (a) shoulder and torso twists without footwork, (b) combining shoulder and torso twists with the polka basic steps without music, and (c) combining shoulder and torso twists with footwork to music. For each part, travel down and back the length of the room.

  a. Stand facing the length of the room. Keep your feet together and stationary. Place your hands on your hips with elbows pointing to the sides. Notice that your shoulders are perpendicular to your forward direction.

  Without moving your feet, bring your left elbow and shoulder forward 90 degrees (moving CW). They should be pointing toward the forward direction.

  Again without moving your feet, bring your right elbow and shoulder forward (moving CCW). Now these should be pointing toward the forward direction.

  Now smoothly repeat both shoulder twists. Notice that you are actually rotating your shoulders a one-quarter turn CW to start, then a half turn CCW (the distance that your back shoulder comes forward), such that your midline faces one side, then the other. One elbow and shoulder always point to the forward direction. One image to consider is opening and shutting a door, because your shoulder and torso twist to open the door one way, then they reverse directions to close the door.

b. Without music, continue repeating your polka steps and freely twisting your torso to bring one elbow and shoulder forward. Check that you are moving your left elbow and foot together, then your right elbow and foot, with each polka basic.

c. Now try both arms and footwork to polka music (see Band 3, Side B, of the soundsheet).

Success Goals =

a. 8 correctly executed shoulder and torso twists

b. 16 correctly executed shoulder and torso twists with polka basics (without music)

c. 16 correctly executed shoulder and torso twists with polka basics (with music)

Your Score =

a. (#) _____ correctly executed twists

b. (#) _____ correctly executed twists and polka basics (without music)

c. (#) _____ correctly executed twists and polka basics (with music)

5. Spot Turn

In preparation for doing a polka turn, you will need to know how to continue turning CW without getting dizzy. This sounds easy, but it is the most difficult variation you will learn in this book. Learning a ''spot'' turn is a helpful answer.

To execute a spot turn, stand at one end of the length of the room. Find a spot at eye level on the wall you are moving toward, and imagine that a string or rope is pulling you toward your spot. At all times, your eyes must focus on your spot.

Without doing any particular footwork, experiment with ways you can both turn and look at your spot as long as possible. Obviously, you'll have to look away at some point, so how can you quickly relocate your spot again?

Notice that your head must turn separately from the rest of your body. Thus, do not turn as if you are a cylinder (with everything turning together). Separate your actions to first let your shoulders turn as far as possible without losing eye contact with your spot. Focus intently on your spot and, when you are looking at your spot from the corners of your eyes, quickly snap your head around to relocate your spot. Then your shoulders can follow (catch up).

Success Goal = 4 correctly executed spot turns without polka footwork or music

Your Score = (#) _____ correctly executed spot turns

6. CW Polka Turn

The ultimate polka variation is the polka turn. You will always turn CW, even as you follow the LOD floor path (CCW around the perimeter of the room). However, at this point, this drill focuses only on traveling the length of the room and back.

Start with your hands on your hips, and select your eye-level spot on the wall far in front of you. Place your weight on your right foot.

Imagine you are traveling along a straight line that moves toward your visual spot. On the upbeat "and" count, hop on your right foot and rotate your body CW 90 degrees to face your side (a one-quarter turn). Your outside shoulder and elbow should now be pointing forward (toward your O.F.). With your left foot, do a triple step forward in this position, keeping your eyes on your spot.

On the next "and" count, hop on your left foot and rotate your shoulders CW 180 degrees (you are now three quarters of the way around). Quickly bring your head around to relocate your spot—which you must locate before your next forward step. Once you relocate your visual spot, you will know exactly where the forward direction is located. Do a triple step with your right foot (keeping your eyes on your spot). Hop on your right foot and rotate your shoulders CW 180 degrees (your outside elbow and shoulder should point toward your O.F. again). Then, continue to repeat two polka basics for each CW turn without music.

When you are ready, try the continuous CW turns to slow polka music. Feel free to stop and start again, especially if you find yourself getting dizzy. The location of your visual spot should be obvious to an observer. So, ask your partner to identify your spot; then you identify your partner's spot.

Success Goals = 2 continuous CW turns (a) without music, then (b) with music

Your Score =

    a. (#) _____ continuous CW turns without music

    b. (#) _____ continuous CW turns with music

Strategy 2: Alter the Timing

There are two basic steps that alter the timing: the magic step in the fox-trot and the single lindy in the swing. Both of these basic steps incorporate a hold or pause in footwork that corresponds to two counts of the music (a 1:2 ratio of footwork actions to rhythmic counts). Even though these basics use the same strategy, they have very different styling features. Each will be addressed.

MAGIC STEP (FOX-TROT BASIC)

There are many variations to the fox-trot, which is an American dance first introduced in 1913 or 1914. The fox-trot got its name from Mr. Harry Fox, a musical comedy star who performed a fast, trotting step to ragtime music in a Ziegfeld musical. As the result of a pub-

licity stunt, Mr. Oscar Duryea, who was a star nightclub performer, was hired to teach this step to the public. However, the original version was too exhausting, so it was modified to alternate four walking steps with eight quick running steps.

Later, Vernon and Irene Castle and other professional dancers helped shape the fox-trot into a smooth, graceful dance. Erect posture and stationary torso and arm movements lend elegance as the partners move around the floor counterclockwise.

An alternative variation, the magic step, was created by the famous dance instructor Arthur Murray. He and his wife, Katherine, used this six-count combination of slow and quick beats (the magic step) in a number of "surprising" ways (covered in Step 9). The counts for the magic step may be called out in the following ways:

Total Counts: Six (accents on even counts)

Rhythmic Counts: 1-2, 3-4, 5, 6

Duration of Steps: Slow, slow, quick, quick

Length of Steps: Long, long, short, short

Direction of Steps: Forward, forward, side, close; or backward, backward, side, close

To execute the basic magic step, start 2 feet from a partner with the man facing the LOD (ready to start with his left foot) and the woman with her back to the LOD (ready to start with her right foot). Stand in correct body alignment with feet in a narrow base (with feet parallel and no more than 2-to-3 inches apart). The magic step can be executed either forward or backward.

To do the magic step forward, take two long, reaching steps (glides) on Counts 1-2 and 3-4. To extend your reach to approximately 18 to 24 inches, bend your trailing knee as you push off. Let the ball of your foot touch the floor during approximately the last 3 inches to create the glide. Keep your feet moving on parallel lines no more than 2 or 3 inches apart.

To add a sharp, 90-degree angle prior to a side step, briefly bring your lead foot up beside your trailing foot without changing weight. Then take a shoulder-width side step with your lead foot on Count 5. Bring your feet together (close) as you transfer your weight onto your trailing foot on Count 6. See Figure 4.4 for the magic step Keys to Success.

To do the magic step backward at this point, reverse the previous directions for executing the forward magic step. Later (in Step 9) you will learn how to switch places with your partner in order for the man to move backward toward the LOD and for the woman to face the LOD.

Fox-Trot Magic Step							
Footwork actions	step	step	side	close			
Rhythmic counts	1 – 2	3 – 4	5	6			
Total counts	1 2	3 4	5	6			
4/4 time signature	1 2	3 4	1	2	3	4	
	>	>	>	>			

Figure 4.4 Keys to Success: Magic Step (Fox-Trot Basic)

Preparation Phase

Man		Woman
Man		**Woman**
____ 1. Correct setup and body alignment		____
____ 2. Feet in a narrow base		____
____ 3. Weight on balls of feet		____
____ 4. Mentally count in fours		____
____ 5. Prepare to move, prior to Count 1		____

Execution
Phase

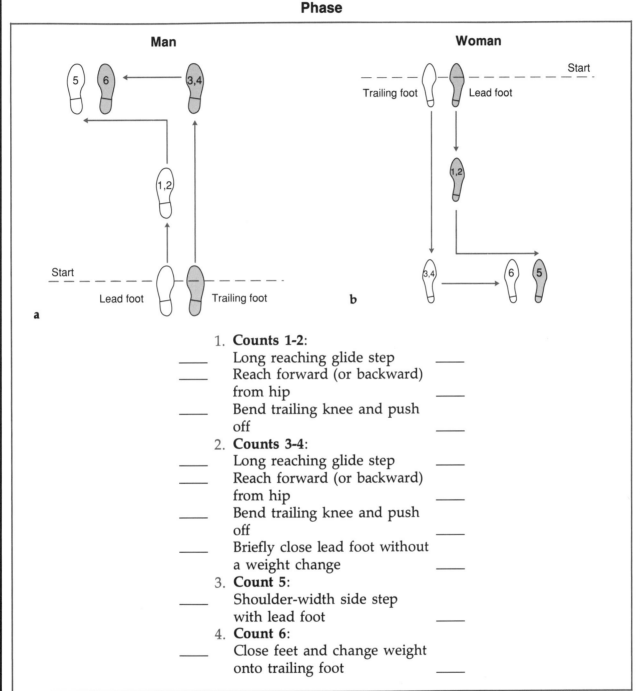

1. **Counts 1-2**:
   ____ Long reaching glide step ____
   ____ Reach forward (or backward) from hip ____
   ____ Bend trailing knee and push off
2. **Counts 3-4**:
   ____ Long reaching glide step ____
   ____ Reach forward (or backward) from hip ____
   ____ Bend trailing knee and push off
   ____ Briefly close lead foot without a weight change ____
3. **Count 5**:
   ____ Shoulder-width side step with lead foot ____
4. **Count 6**:
   ____ Close feet and change weight onto trailing foot ____

**Styling
Phase**

Man		Woman
____ 1.	Smoothly repeat six-count rhythm	
		____
____ 2.	Keep torso and head erect	____
____ 3.	Take long, reaching glide steps on ''slow, slow''	
		____
____ 4.	Crisply take small side step and close on ''quick, quick''	
		____
____ 5.	Effortless, smooth movements	
		____

Drills for the Magic Step (Fox-Trot Basic)

1. Increase Your Reach

Because the beauty of the fox-trot depends so much on the long, reaching glide step, you will need to modify your regular walking step a bit to achieve the proper length. This actual reaching length varies, depending upon your height and your leg length, but it is longer than your regular walking stride.

Place your heels on a line, and stand with your feet 2 to 3 inches apart. Put one end of a yardstick beside you and perpendicular to the line your heels are touching. Take one regular walking step forward, transfer your weight forward onto the ball of your foot, and freeze your position.

Mark where the tip of your toe touches the floor. Use the yardstick to measure the distance from your starting heel position to where the tip of your toe ends. Record this measurement.

Now place your heels back on the line and modify your previous actions by bending your trailing knee and pushing off against the floor with the ball of your trailing foot as you take one step forward. Again transfer your weight onto the ball of your foot and freeze your position. Mark where the tip of your toe ends. Use the yardstick to measure this distance in the same way. Record this measurement.

Compare the two measurements you've just taken. The length of your modified step should be longer.

Success Goal = Awareness of the lengthening effect that a knee bend and pushoff add to your reach

Your Score =

  a. (#) _____ inches reached with regular walking step

  b. (#) _____ inches reached with modified walking step

2. Reach and Glide

This drill combines a long reach and a glide. Use the modified walking step from the previous drill, and during approximately the last 3 inches of your reach, let the ball of your foot glide (slide) along the floor. This glide is characteristic of the fox-trot and helps you avoid stepping on your partner's feet or toes. Notice that your heel does not contact the floor during a reach-and-glide step.

Time your reach-and-glide steps so that your weight transfers onto the ball of your foot with Counts 2 and 4. This gives each reach-and-glide step two counts. It is possible to reach-and-glide in both forward and backward directions.

Do eight reach-and-glides in a forward direction, then repeat going backward. Notice that it is easier to keep your balance once you are in motion.

Success Goals = 8 correctly executed and timed reach-and-glide steps (a) forward, then (b) backward

Your Score =

  a. (#) _____ correctly executed and timed reach-and-glide steps forward

  b. (#) _____ correctly executed and timed reach-and-glide steps backward

3. Basic Magic Step

The magic step combines two reach-and-glide steps with a small side step and a close (review Figure 4.4). Each reach-and-glide step receives two counts, which correspond to the "slow, slow" rhythmic-duration cues. The shoulder-width side step and the close step each receive one count, corresponding to the "quick, quick" rhythmic-duration cues.

Without music, do the magic step forward using a "slow, slow, quick, quick" rhythm. Check that you are traveling forward on the "slow, slow" reaches and sideward (no more than a shoulder-width step) during the "quick, quick" steps. Make sure that you briefly bring your feet together before your side steps.

Then do the magic step backward using the same rhythm. Again, make sure that your footwork actions match the rhythm.

Success Goals = 8 consecutive magic steps, with proper rhythm, (a) forward, then (b) backward

Your Score =

  a. (#) _____ consecutive magic steps forward with proper rhythm

  b. (#) _____ consecutive magic steps backward with proper rhythm

4. Magic Step Forward/Backward Combination

Now you are ready to combine both the forward and the backward magic step into a continuous sequence to slow fox-trot music. This combination is a fun sequence to practice. It will later be modified so that you can effectively travel in the LOD.

Select slow fox-trot music (see Band 4, Side B, of the soundsheet). Do four consecutive magic steps forward, then do four consecutive magic steps backward. Keep all actions fluid and consecutive so that there are no obvious pauses or hesitations.

Success Goal = 2 minutes of consecutive magic steps (4 forward and 4 backward) to slow fox-trot music

Your Score = (#) _____ minutes of consecutive magic steps (4 forward and 4 backward) to slow fox-trot music

SINGLE-LINDY BASIC (SWING)

The first jitterbug step, the shag, was inspired by the boogie-woogie. The shag had a "slow, slow, quick, quick" rhythm that is still used today. The single lindy was the next jitterbug step to evolve. The shag and the single lindy use the same rhythmic pattern and represent early, popular, basic swing steps that are performed to fast, syncopated music. However, the single lindy has evolved to be the most popular version, so it will be described here.

The single-lindy basic takes six counts, just like the triple lindy. However, the execution and tempo for each are different. The triple lindy is used with a slow tempo; the single lindy is used with a fast tempo. Literally, there is not enough time with fast music to execute the three small steps in the triple lindy. The styling points previously discussed with the triple lindy also apply to the single lindy (see Figure 4.1).

The counts for the single lindy may be called out in the following ways:

Total Counts: Six (accents on even counts)

Rhythmic Counts: 1-2, 3-4, 5, 6

Duration of Steps: Slow, slow, quick, quick

Direction of Steps: Forward, backward, ball-change (in place)

To execute the single lindy, stand in proper alignment with your feet parallel and approximately 2 or 3 inches apart. Either set up with a partner or imagine a partner standing beside you, such that the man is on the left and the woman is on the right. Angle your feet and body 45 degrees toward your partner, with body weight on the balls of your feet. Listen for the tempo (it should be fast). Mentally count in fours to the tempo, and prepare to step on any first count with your outside foot.

On Counts 1-2, let your outside shoulder dip slightly and your torso lean forward as you take a small to medium step forward. After you step forward, slightly bend your outside knee. This additional action helps you time your footwork to fit two counts of the music,

Single Lindy							
Footwork actions	step	step	ball	change			
Rhythmic counts	1 – 2	3 – 4	5	6			
Total counts	1 2	3 4	5	6			
4/4 time signature	1 2	3 4	1	2	3	4	
	>	>	>	>			

so that you step on Count 1 and bend your knee on Count 2.

On Counts 3-4, reverse your footwork and styling actions. Thus, let your inside shoulder dip slightly and your torso lean backward as you take a small to medium step backward with your inside foot. After you step back-

ward, slightly bend your inside knee; this again gives you two actions to fit two counts of the music.

The last two counts of the single lindy are the same as the triple lindy— a ball-change on Counts 5 and 6. The Keys to Success for the single lindy are presented in Figure 4.5.

Figure 4.5 Keys to Success: Single-Lindy Basic (Fast Swing Tempo)

Preparation Phase

Man		Woman
____	1. Face front, beside an imaginary partner	____

a

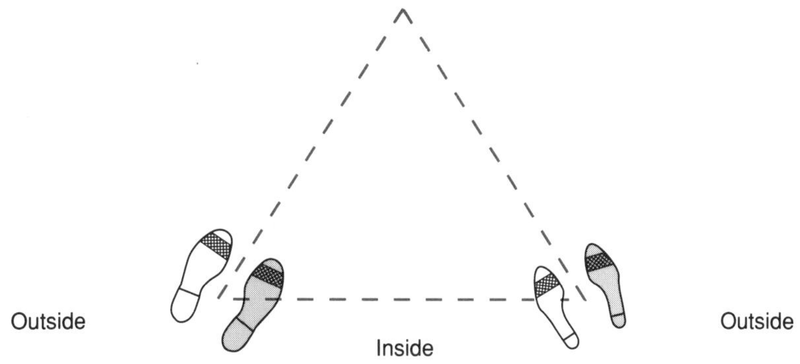

Outside   Inside   Outside

Man		Woman
____	2. Angle feet and body 45 degrees toward partner	____
____	3. Correct body alignment, weight on balls of feet	____
____	4. Listen for fast tempo and rhythm	____
____	5. Mentally count in fours to match tempo	____
____	6. Prepare to step with outside foot on Count 1	____

Execution Phase

Man   **Woman**

b

1. **Counts 1-2**:
   ____ Drop outside shoulder   ____
   ____ Step forward on outside foot
   and bend outside knee   ____
2. **Counts 3-4**:
   ____ Drop inside shoulder   ____
   ____ Step backward on inside foot
   and bend inside knee   ____

c   c

3. **Count 5**:
   ____ Ball   ____
   ____ Torso erect   ____
4. **Count 6**:
   ____ Change   ____
   ____ Torso erect   ____

**Styling
Phase**

Man		Woman
____	1. Maintain consecutive six-count rhythm	____
____	2. Stay within your spot	____
	3. Add jazzy, syncopated styling:	
____	• Torso and shoulder leans on both single steps	____
____	• Upright posture on Counts 5 and 6	____
____	• Keep motions fluid	____
____	• Small ball-change steps	____

Drills for the Single-Lindy (Swing Basic)

1. Single-Lindy Basic

Assume that the music is too fast for you to execute three steps as you did within the triple-lindy basic step. How can you now take a single step on each of the "slow, slow" portions within the swing's basic rhythm (slow, slow, quick, quick)? Experiment with taking only one step forward, then only one step backward. Then, add a ball change. To answer this tempo question, follow the Keys to Success in Figure 4.5 for the single-lindy basic.

   Repeat the single-lindy basic to a self-paced count (gradually increase tempo). Remember to add a torso lean by dropping your outside shoulder as you step forward, then drop your inside shoulder as you step backward. Keep your torso erect on the ball-change counts (5 and 6).

Success Goal = 16 consecutive repetitions of the single-lindy basic with proper styling to a rhythmic count

Your Score = (#) ____ consecutive repetitions of the single-lindy basic with proper styling to a rhythmic count

2. Single-Lindy Basic to Music

Repeat the previous drill to any fast swing music (see Band 5, Side B, of the soundsheet). Make sure that your footwork matches the tempo of the music and that you add proper styling.

Success Goal = 2 minutes of consecutive repetitions of the single lindy with proper styling to a fast swing song

Your Score = (#) _____ minutes of consecutive repetitions of the single lindy with proper styling to a fast swing song

3. Spin 180 Degrees

Without a partner or music, perform the single-lindy basic and experiment with spinning 180 degrees on any Count 2. Take your regular step forward on Count 1, then spin CW or CCW during Count 2. Continue with the rest of the single lindy: Step backward and do the knee bend on Counts 3-4, then do the ball-change on Counts 5 and 6. Make sure that you practice spinning sometimes CW and sometimes CCW on your half turns. Continue practicing until you feel comfortable with all possible half-turn combinations. Your turns should always be executed on the ball of your outside foot.

Then select any fast swing music (see Band 5, Side B, of the soundsheet). Consecutively repeat the single-lindy basic, adding CW and CCW half turns on Count 2 in a random order to the music.

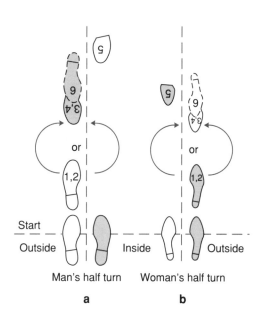

Man's half turn   Woman's half turn

a   b

Success Goals =

  a. 4 consecutive single-lindy basics with a CW half turn on each Count 2

  b. 4 consecutive single-lindy basics with a CCW half turn on each Count 2

  c. 8 consecutive single-lindy basics with CW and CCW half turns (in random order) on each Count 2 to fast swing music

Your Score =

  a. (#) _____ consecutive single-lindy basics with a CW half turn on each Count 2

  b. (#) _____ consecutive single-lindy basics with a CCW half turn on each Count 2

  c. (#) _____ consecutive single-lindy basics with CW and CCW half turns (in random order) on each Count 2 to fast swing music

Uneven-Rhythm Dance Basics
Keys to Success Checklists

The dance basics with uneven rhythms challenge you not only to execute correctly, but also to add the unique styling that distinguishes and gives personality to the various social dances. The Success Goals have given you quantitative measures of your performance of five packaged basics. To measure your technique qualitatively, ask your teacher or another trained observer to rate both your execution and your use of appropriate styling, according to these checklists:

- Triple lindy (see Figure 4.1)
- Cha-cha (see Figure 4.2)
- Polka (see Figure 4.3)

- Magic step (see Figure 4.4)
- Single lindy (see Figure 4.5)

As a self-test, ask a partner to randomly play five different songs (one song for each of the dance styles just listed) as you identify the correct dance type and execute the appropriate dance basic. Or you could play Bands 1 through 5, Side B, of the soundsheet.

How you move is very important within social dance. Once you can properly execute and add the appropriate styling features to these five basic steps, you are ready to learn the remaining three packaged basic steps (in Step 5).

Step 5 Even-Rhythm Dance Basics

There are three basic dance steps with even rhythms: the fox-trot box step, the waltz box step, and the double lindy. Each of these uses the same strategy for footwork execution—match one walking step or action with each whole count of the music (a 1:1 ratio). All three basics are to be practiced without touching a partner, yet being aware of your partner's position.

WHY ARE THE EVEN-RHYTHM DANCE BASICS IMPORTANT?

The even-rhythm dance basics have a repetitive, soothing quality about them that makes them very pleasant to do. They are also helpful alternatives when you are selecting the basic that best fits a given tempo, and when you begin to plan routines that adjust to the flow of traffic. Lastly, you can add to your dance styles with the waltz, which is usually the second most popular music played in an evening.

Strategy 3: Match an Action With Each Count

The footwork execution strategy of matching an action with each count may or may not involve a weight change with each whole count of the music. All of the basics presented here use this strategy, which greatly simplifies their execution and makes it easy to remember how to do them.

FOX-TROT BOX STEP

All of the fox-trot styling descriptions from Step 4 also apply to the fox-trot box step. However, the box step's rhythm is even (with one action per count), whereas the magic step's rhythm was uneven because you had to alter your timing to take only one reaching step within two counts of the music during the "slow, slow" rhythm cues. In comparison, you should find that the fox-trot box step is very easy to learn.

The fox-trot box step uses eight counts. These counts may be called out in the following ways:

> *Total Counts*: Eight (accents on even counts)
> *Rhythmic Counts*: 1, 2, 3, 4; 1, 2, 3, 4, or 1, 2, 3, 4, 5, 6, 7, 8
> *Duration of Steps*: Quick, quick, quick, quick (both halves)
> *Direction of Steps*: Forward, touch, side, together; backward, touch, side, together (backward half)

Although this basic step is called the "box" step, imagine that you are making a rectangular (rather than square) box on the floor. On Count 1 of the forward half-box, reach forward with your left foot, and glide the ball of your foot during the last 3 inches of your step (and change your weight). On Count 2, bring the ball of your right foot beside the ball of your left foot to touch, but do not change your weight. Then continue moving your right foot directly sideward (notice that your right foot traces a 90-degree angle along the floor). On Count 3, step to your right side onto your right foot (your side step should be no more than the width of your shoulders). On Count 4, bring your left foot beside your right to close, and change your weight onto your left foot.

The backward half of the fox-trot box step starts with your right foot. Reversing your previous actions, take a long, reaching glide step backward on Count 1. On Count 2, bring the ball of your left foot beside the ball of your right foot to touch, but do not change weight.

Fox-Trot Box Step	Forward half				Backward half			
Footwork actions	fwd	touch	side	close	bwd	touch	side	close
Rhythmic counts	1	2	3	4	1	2	3	4
Total counts	1	2	3	4	5	6	7	8
4/4 time signature	1	2	3	4	1	2	3	4
	>		>		>		>	

Then continue moving your left foot directly sideward to step (on Count 3) onto your left foot (both feet should be no more than shoulder-width apart). On Count 4, bring your right foot beside your left to close, and change your weight onto your right foot.

As an alternative, you can move through the narrow base position on Count 2 without actually doing a touch. When substituting this action for the "touch," the duration of your steps becomes SQQ.

Facing each other and moving simultaneously, the man starts with his left foot (to do the half-box forward, then backward) as the woman starts with her right foot (to do the half-box backward, then forward). See Figure 5.1 for the fox-trot box-step technique Keys to Success.

Figure 5.1   Keys to Success: Fox-Trot Box Step

Preparation Phase

Man		Woman
____ 1. Torso and head erect		____
____ 2. Weight on balls of feet		____
____ 3. Listen for tempo		____
____ 4. Mentally count in fours		____
____ 5. Anticipate stepping on Count 1		____

Execution Phase

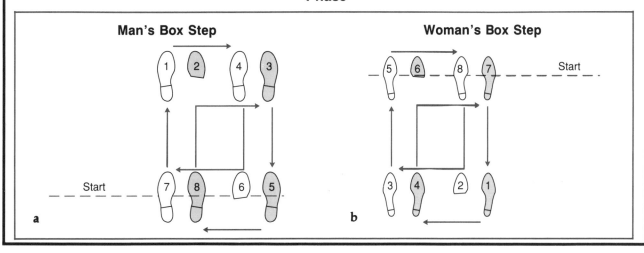

	Forward Half-Box (Man Starts Here)		Backward Half-Box (Woman Starts Here)
1.	**Count 1:** Long, reaching glide step forward with left foot ____	1.	**Count 1:** Long, reaching glide step backward with right foot ____
2.	**Count 2:** Touch ball of right foot beside left foot ____	2.	**Count 2:** Touch ball of left foot beside right foot ____
3.	**Count 3:** Short side step onto ball of right foot ____	3.	**Count 3:** Short side step onto ball of left foot ____
4.	**Count 4:** Close ____	4.	**Count 4:** Close ____

**Styling
Phase**

Man		Woman
____	1. Smoothly connect both halves	
____	2. Keep torso and head erect	____
____	3. Long, reaching step on Count 1	____
____	4. Shoulder-width side step	____
____	5. Rectangular (not square) box traced on floor	____

Drills for the Fox-Trot Box Step

1. Fox-Trot Box Step

Challenge yourself with the following problem: Without a partner, experiment to modify the fox-trot magic step (from Step 4) as follows: Can you now take only one long, reach-and-glide step and then add the side step? Can you repeat this modification while moving both forward (start with your left foot) and backward (start with your right foot)? If so, you are performing the fox-trot box step.

If this problem solving is too difficult for you, review the footwork actions in Figure 5.1.

Notice that the full box step takes eight counts and combines both the forward half-box and the backward half-box. Without music, count in eights, and combine both of these half-boxes. Check that you consecutively match eight actions with eight counts (i.e., do one action with each whole count).

Success Goal = 16 consecutive repetitions of the fox-trot box step, matching one action with each whole count

Your Score = (#) ___ consecutive repetitions of the fox-trot box step, matching one action with each whole count

2. *Fox-Trot Box Step to Music*

Repeat the previous drill to any slow fox-trot music (see Band 4, Side B). Make sure that you add the following styling points to match each count of the music:

- Long, reaching glide step on Counts 1 and 5
- Feet briefly touch on Counts 2 and 6
- Small (shoulder-width) step directly to the side on Counts 3 and 7
- Close (bring feet together and change your weight) on Counts 4 and 8

Remember to keep your head and shoulders upright throughout.

Success Goal = 2 consecutive minutes of the fox-trot box step, with proper styling, to slow fox-trot music

Your Score = (#) ___ consecutive minutes of the fox-trot box step, with proper styling, to slow fox-trot music

3. *Face a Partner*

Without touching, stand facing a partner approximately 2 feet away. Take turns with your partner counting in fours and cuing when to begin moving (e.g., ''1, 2, 3, 4; 1, 2, ready, begin''). One partner starts with the forward half-box as the other partner starts with the backward half-box. You will end up reversing both the footwork and directions of each other.

a. Double-check that your footwork creates a rectangular shape on the floor (due to your long first step and small side steps). After 16 consecutive box steps, reverse starting points with your partner and repeat.

b. Repeat part a to any slow fox-trot music (see Band 4, Side B). Make sure that you are using proper styling and smoothly connecting all steps into one continuous flow of action, as well as crisply executing one action with each count of the music.

Success Goals =

a. 16 consecutive repetitions of the fox-trot box step, facing a partner (without music)

b. 2 minutes of consecutive repetitions of the fox-trot box step with proper styling, facing a partner, to slow fox-trot music

Your Score =

a. (#) ____ consecutive repetitions of the fox-trot box step, facing a partner (without music)

b. (#) ____ minutes of consecutive repetitions of the fox-trot box step with proper styling, facing a partner, to slow fox-trot music

WALTZ BOX STEP

The waltz is a smooth dance that became popular after two Austrian composers, Johann Strauss and Franz Lanner, created beautiful waltz music in the 1800s. In 3/4 time, waltz music accentuates the first count. This first-count musical accent is further accented by both the footwork execution (the longer step) and step variations (changing directions). The waltz is characterized by erect posture, closed dance position (described in Step 6), wavelike rise-and-fall motion, and turns.

Due to three different tempos of waltz music, there are three different styles of waltz. The slow to moderate tempo (30 to 40 measures per minute) is appropriate for the American waltz. The American waltz is popular at cotillions and elaborate social balls. The fast tempo (50 to 60 measures per minute) is appropriate for the Viennese waltz, which incorporates consecutive turns, both CW and CCW; the Viennese waltz is challenging because of its speed and consecutive left-then-right turns. The third style of waltz, the international waltz, began in England in the 1800s and incorporates very complicated movements at a moderate tempo. Only the American waltz will be described, because it is the easiest to learn—starting with its basic box step.

The waltz box step takes six counts. These counts may be called out in the following ways:

Total Counts: Six (accent on Counts 1 and 4)

Rhythmic Counts: 1, 2, 3, 1, 2, 3; or 1, 2, 3, 4, 5, 6

Duration of Steps: Slow, slow, slow (both halves)

Length of Steps: Long, short, short (both halves)

Direction of Steps: Forward, side, together (forward half); backward, side, together (backward half)

To execute the waltz box step, imagine a rectangular box shape drawn on the floor. The goal is to step on each corner of the rectangular box while grouping your steps in threes to coincide with the 3/4-time music. Match your longest step (either forward or backward) with the first count of the music. Match your short side step with the second count, and close your feet together on the third count. Both an action and a weight change occur on each count. A completed waltz box step takes six total counts: three counts for each half.

Notice that you can now eliminate the "touch" action that was used in the fox-trot box step. To do this, your second step must travel directly to the diagonal corner to take a side step on Count 2. The fastest way to get to the side step in one count is to move your foot in a straight line, as if bisecting a rectangle into two triangles (see Figure 5.2).

Most characteristic of the waltz is a smooth,

Waltz Box Step	Forward half			Backward half		
Footwork actions	fwd	side	close	bwd	side	close
Rhythmic counts	1	2	3	1	2	3
Total counts	1	2	3	4	5	6
3/4 time signature	1	2	3	1	2	3
	>			>		

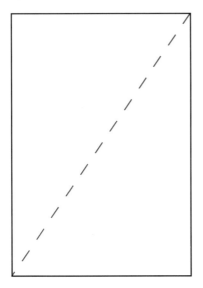

Figure 5.2 Travel along the diagonal line on Count 2 of the waltz box step.

fluid motion with a subtle rise-and-fall action. This action results from (a) slightly bending your pushoff knee as you take a long, reaching glide on Count 1; (b) transferring your weight higher onto the ball of your foot as you take a side step on Count 2; and (c) gently lowering your heels as you close your feet together on Count 3. A forced, artificial rise-and-fall action will detract from your performance. It is better to focus on proper execution first; then you can let a *subtle* lowering and rising of your entire body naturally occur. Figure 5.3 shows the Keys to Success for performing the waltz box step.

Figure 5.3 Keys to Success: Waltz Box Step

Preparation Phase

Man		Woman
____ 1. Correct body alignment		____
____ 2. Weight on balls of feet		____
____ 3. Listen for tempo		____
____ 4. Mentally count in threes		____
____ 5. Anticipate stepping on Count 1		____

Execution Phase

Man's Box Step

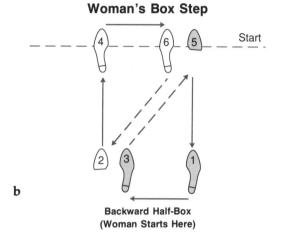

a

Start

Forward Half-Box
(Man Starts Here)

Woman's Box Step

Start

b

Backward Half-Box
(Woman Starts Here)

1. **Count 1:**
   Long, reaching glide forward with left foot ____
2. **Count 2:**
   Shoulder-width side step onto ball of right foot ____
3. **Count 3:**
   Close (bring ball of left foot beside ball of right foot) ____

1. **Count 1:**
   Long, reaching glide backward with right foot ____
2. **Count 2:**
   Shoulder-width side step onto ball of left foot ____
3. **Count 3:**
   Close (ball of right foot beside ball of left foot) ____

Styling Phase

Man		Woman
____	1. Smoothly connect both half-boxes	____
____	2. Match a long step with the first count of each measure	____
____	3. Small side steps	____
____	4. Make a rectangular (rather than square) box shape	____
____	5. Maintain erect upper torso and head (regal bearing)	____
	6. Subtle rise-and-fall:	
____	• Slightly bend your pushoff knee on Count 1	____
____	• Slightly lift onto balls of your feet on Count 2	____
____	• Slightly lower body weight on Count 3	____

Drills for the Waltz Box Step

1. Waltz Box Step

Challenge yourself with the following problem: How can you create a rectangular box shape on the floor (as you did with the fox-trot box step), yet use only six total counts (three for each half of the waltz box step—versus four for each half of the fox-trot box step)?

To answer these questions, follow the Keys to Success in Figure 5.3 for the waltz box step. Repeat these actions both forward and backward, blending both halves into a continuous box step. Make sure that you are making a rectangular (rather than square) box shape on the floor.

In comparison with the fox-trot box step, now you should be eliminating the inward movement of the fox-trot box step's Count 2. Because there is literally not enough time for that touch movement in the waltz's 3/4 time signature, your second step needs to cut diagonally across the rectangle to the side step on Count 2. You may have to practice a bit to remove the fox-trot's Count 2 action.

Success Goal =   16 consecutive repetitions of the waltz box step, matching one action with each count

Your Score =   (#) _____ consecutive repetitions, matching one action with each count

2. Waltz Box Step to Music

Without a partner, repeat the previous drill to any slow waltz music (see Band 6, Side B, of the soundsheet). Keep each of the waltz box step's six counts connected with the music and continuous. Start with the basic footwork actions in the following order: forward, side, close; backward, side, close.

Use either or both of the following cues to help you smoothly blend all counts: ''reach, side, close'' or ''long, short, short.''

Then repeat this drill, reversing the order: backward, side, close; forward, side, close.

Success Goals =   2 minutes of consecutive waltz box steps with proper rhythm, to slow waltz music, (a) starting with the forward half, then (b) starting with the backward half

Your Score =

a. (#) _____ minutes of consecutive waltz box steps with proper rhythm (starting with forward half)

b. (#) _____ minutes of consecutive waltz box steps with proper rhythm (starting with backward half)

3. Face a Partner

a. Without touching, stand facing a partner approximately 2 feet away. Take turns with your partner counting in threes and cuing when to begin moving (e.g., "1, 2, 3; 1, ready, begin"). One partner starts with the forward half-box as the other partner starts with the backward half-box.

   Double-check that your footwork creates a rectangular shape on the floor (due to your long first step and small side steps). After 16 consecutive box steps, reverse starting points with your partner and repeat. Keep your torso and head erect throughout, and avoid any tendency to watch either your own or your partner's feet.

b. Repeat the previous drill to any slow waltz music (see Band 6, Side B, of the soundsheet). Make sure that you are using proper styling and smoothly connecting all steps into one continuous flow of action with the music.

Success Goals =

a. 16 consecutive repetitions of the waltz box step, facing a partner (without music)

b. 2 minutes of consecutive repetitions of the waltz box step with proper styling, facing a partner, to slow waltz music

Your Score =

a. (#) _____ consecutive repetitions of the waltz box step, facing a partner (without music)

b. (#) _____ minutes of consecutive repetitions of the waltz box step with proper styling, facing a partner, to slow waltz music

DOUBLE-LINDY BASIC (SWING)

The double lindy became popular when syncopated rock-and-roll music was introduced during the late 1940s, and its popularity continued through the 1950s and 1960s. It is very adaptable to moderate and some fast tempos. Characteristic styling points are the same as those described in Step 4 for the triple lindy. Remember to lean your shoulder and torso either forward or backward just before taking a step, but keep your torso and head upright on the last two counts.

The double lindy takes six counts. These counts may be called out in the following ways:

Total Counts: Six (accents on even counts)

Rhythmic Counts: 1-2, 3-4, 5, 6

Duration of Steps: Quick-quick, quick-quick, quick, quick

Direction of Steps: Forward, backward, ball-change (in place)

To execute the double lindy, stand in proper alignment, with your feet parallel and 2 or 3 inches apart. Set up with either a partner or an imaginary partner standing beside you (with the man on the left and the woman on the right). Angle your feet and body 45 degrees inward toward your partner. Move your body weight onto the balls of your feet. Listen for the tempo (it should be moderate). Mentally count in fours to the tempo, and prepare to step on any first count with your outside foot.

The double lindy differs from both the triple lindy and the single lindy in that it uses two footwork actions for each of its forward and backward portions. Thus, much as if you were doing a Native American war dance, moving slightly forward, dig the ball of your

Double Lindy								
Footwork actions	toe	heel	toe	heel	ball	change		
Rhythmic counts	1	2	3	4	5	6		
Total counts	1	2	3	4	5	6		
4/4 time signature	1	2 >	3	4 >	1	2 >	3	4 >

outside foot down on Count 1, and drop your outside heel on Count 2. Moving slightly backward with your inside foot, dig the ball of your inside foot down on Count 3, and drop your inside heel on Count 4.

Counts 5 and 6 are the same ball-change steps that were used with both the triple lindy and the single lindy. Make sure you place the ball of your outside foot 2 inches behind the heel of your inside foot as you simultaneously lift your inside knee to raise your foot barely off the floor (Count 5). Then step down on your inside foot without changing its location (Count 6). The moderately fast tempo of the music necessitates small steps or your timing will be slower than the music.

Many variations are possible within the double lindy's six-count rhythm, including using an alternating touch-step (which will be used in Step 12) instead of ball-heel action for the first four counts. Ball-heel action is summarized in Figure 5.4.

Figure 5.4 Keys to Success: Double-Lindy Basic (Moderate Swing Tempo)

Preparation Phase

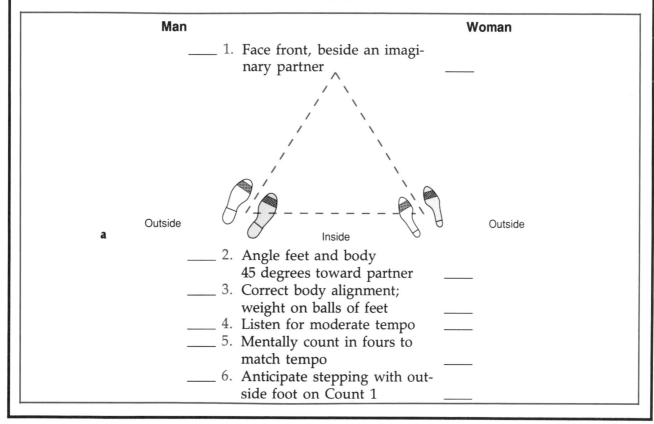

Man · Woman

_____ 1. Face front, beside an imaginary partner _____

Outside · Inside · Outside

a

_____ 2. Angle feet and body 45 degrees toward partner _____

_____ 3. Correct body alignment; weight on balls of feet _____

_____ 4. Listen for moderate tempo _____

_____ 5. Mentally count in fours to match tempo _____

_____ 6. Anticipate stepping with outside foot on Count 1 _____

Execution
Phase

Man

b

Woman

b

1. **Count 1**:
____ Drop outside shoulder ____
____ Dig ball of outside foot ____
2. **Count 2**:
____ Drop outside heel ____
3. **Count 3**:
____ Drop inside shoulder ____
____ Dig ball of inside foot ____
4. **Count 4**:
____ Drop inside heel ____
5. **Count 5**:
____ Ball ____
____ Torso erect ____
6. **Count 6**:
____ Change ____
____ Torso erect ____

Styling
Phase

Man   **Woman**

____ 1. Continuously repeat six-count
      rhythm   ____
____ 2. Use small steps throughout   ____
____ 3. Stay within your spot   ____
      4. Add jazzy, syncopated
         styling:
____   • Torso and shoulder leans
          with ball-heels   ____
____   • Upright posture on Counts
          5 and 6   ____
____   • Percussive heel-drops
          match music accents   ____

Drills for the Double-Lindy Basic (Swing)

1. Double-Lindy Basic

Some music is too fast for you to execute three steps as you did with the triple-lindy basic, but too slow to do the single-lindy basic easily. The third swing basic option, the double lindy, is especially appropriate for moderate-tempo swing songs.

Review the Keys to Success in Figure 5.4 for the double-lindy execution techniques. Practice matching all six footwork actions to the six-count rhythm. Make sure that you drop your shoulder appropriately.

Success Goal = 16 consecutive repetitions of the double-lindy basic with proper styling to a rhythmic count

Your Score = (#) _____ consecutive repetitions of the double-lindy basic with proper styling to a rhythmic count

2. Double-Lindy Basic to Music

Repeat the previous drill to any moderate swing music (see Band 7, Side B). Make sure that your footwork matches the tempo of the music, and that you mirror your partner's torso leans to each side, then straighten torso (without touching).

Success Goal = 2 minutes of consecutive repetition of the double lindy with proper styling to a moderate swing song

Your Score = (#) _____ minutes of consecutive repetitions of the double lindy with proper styling to a moderate swing song

3. Footwork for Half Turns

As you have previously done with both the triple lindy and the single lindy, you can turn 180 degrees with the double lindy, too. Without a partner or music, dig the ball of your outside foot forward on Count 1, and spin on the ball of your outside foot prior to your outside heel drop on Count 2. Then do your ball-heel actions backward with your inside foot, and the regular ball-change steps on Counts 5 and 6.

Practice turning only CW, then only CCW on your half turns. Your turns should always be executed on the ball of your outside foot.

With music, do your CW and CCW turns

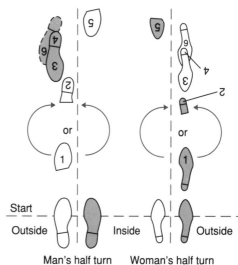

Start

Outside | Inside | Outside

Man's half turn | Woman's half turn

a | b

in a random order. Select any moderate- to fast-tempo swing music (see Bands 7 and 5, Side B, of the soundsheet). Continue practicing until you feel comfortable with all possible half-turn combinations.

Success Goals =

a. 4 consecutive double-lindy basics with a CW half turn just before Count 2

b. 4 consecutive double-lindy basics with a CCW half turn just before Count 2

c. 8 consecutive double-lindy basics with CW and CCW half turns (in random order) just before Count 2, to moderate swing music

Your Score =

a. (#) ____ consecutive double-lindy basics with CW half turns

b. (#) ____ consecutive double-lindy basics with CCW half turns

c. (#) ____ consecutive double-lindy basics with CW and CCW half turns (in random order) just before Count 2, to moderate swing music

Even-Rhythm Dance Basics Keys to Success Checklists

The dance basics with even rhythms challenge you to both execute correctly and add the unique styling that distinguishes the various social dances. The Success Goals have given you quantitative measures of your performance of three more packaged basics. To measure your technique qualitatively, ask your teacher or another trained observer to rate both your execution and your use of appropriate styling according to the following checklists:

• Fox-trot box step (see Figure 5.1)

• Waltz box step (see Figure 5.3)
• Double lindy (see Figure 5.4)

As a self-test, ask a partner to randomly play three different songs (one song for each of the dance styles just listed) as you identify the correct dance type and execute the appropriate basic step. Or you could play the first three song segments on Band 2, Side A, of the soundsheet. With the swing selection, you will need to decide whether the triple lindy, single lindy, or double lindy best fits the tempo—it is your preference!

Step 6 Communicating With Your Partner

It is very natural, before dancing with a partner, to have some uncertainties, such as: How should you ask a partner to dance? Who asks whom to dance? What do you do if a partner does not want to dance? What are the correct dance positions for each dance style? Will your partner know how to give the proper leads or how to follow? What do you do if your partner doesn't know the basic step? What do you do if your partner criticizes you? You can be more in control of these uncertainties if you know how to communicate effectively in a social dance setting.

Basically, there are two ways of communicating with your partner, verbally and nonverbally. Both ways contribute to making the "social" in social dancing a more pleasant experience. Verbal communication includes both knowing and practicing proper ballroom etiquette, as well as promoting and practicing a respectful attitude toward your partner. Nonverbal communication includes both general and specific tips for following and leading, for the correct partner positions, and for the transitions used to connect the basic partner positions used in the five dance styles covered in this book.

WHY IS IT IMPORTANT TO COMMUNICATE WITH YOUR PARTNER?

It is said that good communication is made up of the following components:

- 7 percent words
- 38 percent voice quality
- 55 percent body language

Thus, your actions literally speak louder than your words!

In addition, we all need to give and receive positive strokes. If you are polite and respectful of your partner's space, then she or he will be more likely to treat you in the same manner. There are very traditional etiquette rules that operate within social dancing. Once you know these rules, you will be ready to "play the game" too.

PROPER ETIQUETTE RULES

Ballroom dancing etiquette is very traditional. The following rules are typically found in sponsored, nondate events:

- It is good manners for the man to ask a woman to dance rather than stand on the sidelines watching.
- The man politely asks the woman to dance.
- The woman graciously accepts. (If the woman truly does not want to dance, she can say so, but she should not dance with another partner until that particular dance is over.)
- There is a "no monopolizing" rule, meaning that the woman may excuse herself after two successive dances to provide the man an opportunity to ask another partner. (This rule encourages mixing and more opportunities for all to dance.)
- The man should not cut in on a dancing couple without first asking any woman who is not dancing whether she would like to dance.
- Be considerate of your partner. (Avoid giving helpful hints or criticizing or dancing for the benefit of onlookers.)
- Be considerate of other couples. (Avoid difficult steps when the floor is crowded, or steering your partner around the floor like you are driving a car.)
- The woman should let the man lead.
- The woman should not let her arm rest heavily on the man's arm.
- Women should not huddle in groups,

which makes it harder for the men to ask them to dance.
- Avoid singing, counting out loud, or chewing gum to the music as you dance.

These are examples of how the man can politely ask a partner to dance:

- "May I have this dance?"
- "Would you like to dance?"

These are examples of how the woman can graciously accept an invitation:

- "Certainly."
- "Yes, you may."
- "Yes, I would like to."
- "I would love to."

The main advantage of these rules is that they encourage positive interactions and continual interchanges. The atmosphere is similar to a group date, because the group members constantly interrelate throughout an evening of dancing, with each member fulfilling the role of a good host or hostess. Here are some of the courtesies everyone should observe:

- Introduce yourself, and introduce other people who do not know each other.
- Point out some commonalities to encourage communication.
- Dance with many different partners.
- The men escort their partners back to where they asked them to dance.
- Both partners thank each other for the dance.
- Offer an apology if you accidently bump someone.
- Avoid giving instructions on the dance floor.
- Inconspicuously and gently lead a partner through an unknown step.
- Thank the official host or hostess at the end of the evening.

BASIC PARTNER POSITIONS

There are six basic partner positions that typically are used in social dancing. These include the shine position (described in Step 4), two-hands joined position, one-hand joined position, closed position, semiopen position, and inside-hands joined position (see Figure 6.1).

Figure 6.1 Keys to Success: Basic Partner Positions

Two-Hands Joined Position

Cha-Cha	Swing
____ 1. Stand facing partner	____
____ 2. Palms face down	____
____ 3. Man separates thumb and fingers	____

Cha-Cha	Swing

a

a

4. Man's palms down with elbows away from body ____

4. Man's palms up with elbows close to body ____

____ 5. Woman keeps palms down ____

b

b

6. Man moves closer ____
7. His thumbs in her palms ____
8. His fingers on top of her hands ____

6. Man moves closer ____
7. His thumbs on the top of her fingers ____
8. His fingers in her palm ____

One-Hand Joined Position

Cha-Cha	Swing

____ 1. Stand facing partner ____
____ 2. Palms face down ____
____ 3. Man separates thumb and fingers ____

Cha-Cha

c

4. Man's palm down with elbow away from body ____
5. Man moves closer ____
6. His thumb in her palm ____
7. His fingers on top of her hand ____

Swing

c

4. Man's palm up with elbow close to body ____
5. Man moves closer ____
6. His thumb on the top of her fingers ____
7. His fingers in her palm ____

Closed Position

Woman   **Man**

d

____ 1. Stand facing partner ____
____ 2. Man moves a half step to his left ____
____ 3. Look over partner's right shoulder (as partner's height permits) ____
____ 4. Feet parallel and 2 to 3 inches apart ____

Woman **Man**

e

5. Curve left elbow as an extension from the shoulders ____
6. Place left arm on top of man's curved right arm ____
7. Place little-finger side of left hand slightly in front of man's right shoulder ____
8. Curve right elbow as an extension from shoulders ____
9. Right-hand palm down ____

5. Curve right elbow as an extension from shoulders ____
6. Place right-hand palm and fingers just below woman's left shoulder blade ____
7. Keep right-hand fingers together ____
8. Curve left elbow as an extension from shoulders ____
9. Left-hand palm down ____

____10. Interlock man's left and woman's right hand ____
____11. Maintain this "frame" ____

Semiopen Position

LOD Dances (Waltz, Fox-Trot, Polka)	Swing

f

f

_____ 1. Stand beside partner (man on left, woman on right) _____

_____ 2. Angle feet and body 45 degrees toward partner _____

_____ 3. Man places his right-hand palm and fingers below woman's left shoulder blade _____

_____ 4. Man curves right elbow _____

_____ 5. Woman places curved left arm barely on man's curved right arm _____

_____ 6. Woman places little-finger side of hand in front of his shoulder _____

_____ 7. Both extend outside arms, keeping palms facing down _____

8. Interlock hands with the woman's hand on top _____

8. Man rotates left thumb CW to be on top of woman's fingers _____

Inside-Hands Joined
Position

Man   **Woman**

_____ 1. Stand side by side (man on
left, woman on right)   _____

g    h

2. Man extends right arm
and hand toward
partner _____

2. Woman places left palm
in partner's palm _____

_____ 3. Grasp hands   _____
_____ 4. Outside hands on hips   _____

Detecting Basic
Partner-Position Errors

You and your partner may be able to do the basic partner positions while standing stationary. However, if you do not maintain the appropriate posture while dancing, you will create errors. All of the following errors make it more difficult to either lead or follow a partner.

ERROR

CORRECTION

1. During a forward lead from a closed position, either only elbows move (a) or only shoulders (b) rather than both elbows and shoulders moving.

a b

1. Both partners need to "connect" elbows and shoulders to move together rather than in isolation. Maintaining this frame is especially important in the closed and semiopen positions.

2. Elbows are allowed to extend (straighten) during either the two-hands joined position or the one-hand joined position (in swing). Straightening your elbows throws your head and upper torso backward, throwing you off balance, and slowing down your timing with the music.

2. Keep elbows at 90-degree angles, close to sides of body, and only let your elbow(s) range 45 degrees forward or backward from the original 90 degrees. Thus, you need to alternately relax and tense your arm muscles (like a shock absorber) to stay within the desired range.

ERROR	CORRECTION
3. Either too little or too much force is used when leading or following.	3. The man needs to provide firm leads without literally pushing and pulling his partner. The woman needs to hold the weight of her own arms in a position to both receive and respond to the man's subtle leads. The goal is to work in unison with the music and make the actions seem effortless.
4. The extended arms, in either the closed dance position or the semiopen position, pump up and down in time with the music.	4. Any pumping actions greatly detract from the styling of a dance. Typically, the elegance of the fox-trot and the waltz is enhanced by maintaining an upright, and firm upper body.

GENERAL TIPS FOR FOLLOWING A PARTNER

A good "follower" in dance terms recognizes the appropriate leads and direction changes to work in unison with her partner. To do this, you need to be ready to respond to any direction lead. However, you also need to avoid anticipating a particular lead, because then you, and not your partner, will be leading. The man gives the leads—at least on the dance floor!

One tip is to focus your attention on your partner's shoulders, because they indicate direction changes. Use your peripheral vision to watch the man's shoulders. Avoid the habit of watching your own feet, which indicates that you need more practice without a partner to ingrain the basic steps. As you learn the specific leads, become aware of the amount of pressure (nonverbal feedback) given by your partner. It is very difficult to lead (or follow) someone who has either very rigid or very limp ("spaghetti") arms.

A major adjustment for the woman is to reverse her footwork actions from her partner's footwork. Typically, dance cues are given for the man, with the assumption that the woman reverses everything. For example, to move in a closed dance position in the LOD, the man starts forward with his left foot, while the woman starts backward with her right

foot. This adjustment permits both partners to travel in the LOD.

GENERAL TIPS FOR LEADING A PARTNER

To be a good leader, you need to know your basic steps so well that you can do them without thinking about them. So, self-test yourself on all the basic steps (in Steps 4 and 5)—they must be done automatically! When you can repeat the basic steps to the music without looking at your feet, you will be able to think about other things, like how to lead, when to signal a lead, and how to make transitions to combine steps into short sequences.

Social dancing involves a give-and-take. Balanced interactions between partners can create beautiful, fluid, movements. Both partners must work together to ensure that this happens. As mentioned earlier, the man should not forcibly push or pull his partner into various positions, yet he also needs to communicate firm, obvious leads.

What is most difficult about leading is knowing how much force to use and when to give a particular lead. In general, the leads involve gentle pressure in various directions: forward, backward, sideward, rotating, and turning; but a "lead" typically comprises a combination of actions. For example, the man can initiate a rotation with his partner by rotating his shoulders either CW or CCW, which involves both a push and a pull as well as maintaining a solid frame. However, unless the woman also maintains a firm frame, these correct actions may be misinterpreted.

All leads must be given before any actual movement, so that you can give your partner enough time to respond. A lead is a nonverbal signal to help both partners match footwork with Count 1 of the music. The woman's footwork actions are typically reversed. Thus, in a closed dance position, a lead to move forward signals that the man is going to start forward with his left foot and that the woman should start backward with her right foot. Specific leads for each dance style are described in the following drill sections.

Drills for Cha-Cha Leads, Transitions, and Short Combinations

1. Fingertip Pressure

Stand facing a partner with your feet together, elbows and wrists bent, and palms facing your partner with your fingertips touching. Adjust the height of your hands and arms to be comfortably below your shoulders yet above your waists.

Remain stationary, and take turns initiating gentle pressure against your partner's fingertips. Reciprocate your partner's pressure such that neither partner's fingertips move more than 3 to 6 inches. Take turns initiating a press that moves both hands in the following opposing directions:

- Forward and backward
- Left and right
- Up and down
- Rotating CW and CCW

Success Goal = 4 opposing directions gently led with fingertip pressure

Your Score = (#) _____ opposing directions successfully led

2. Cha-Cha Forward and Backward Leads

Start in a two-hands joined position with the man's thumb in the woman's palms and his fingers on the back of her hands (see Figures 6.1 a, b). Without music and prior to Count 1, the man gently presses both hands slightly forward. Both partners do the cha-cha basic as the man either presses forward or pulls back slightly to correspond with his forward and backward cha-cha motions. Do at least sixteen continuous repetitions of the cha-cha basic with correctly timed forward and backward leads to counts.

Repeat with slow cha-cha music. Move in unison with your partner to smoothly connect both the forward and backward direction changes within the cha-cha basic to the music.

Success Goals = 16 continuous repetitions of the cha-cha basic with correctly timed forward and backward leads (a) without music, then (b) with music

Your Score =

a. (#) _____ continuous repetitions with correctly timed leads (without music)

b. (#) _____ continuous repetitions with correctly timed leads (with music)

3. Shine Position to Two-Hands Joined Position Transitions

Start in a shine position. Without music, do the cha-cha basic step without touching your partner. On any of the man's cha-cha-cha steps forward, the man moves closer to his partner. With his thumb and fingers separated, the man can slide his thumb underneath the woman's downward-facing palms whenever he gets close enough. Continue the cha-cha basic. The man gently presses his fingers and thumb together to grasp the woman's hands (see Figure 6.1 a, b). Then he gently presses or pulls with both hands to correspond with either his forward or his backward cha-cha motions. To get back to the shine position, the man lets go of the woman's hands and moves slightly apart.

Without music, do at least six smooth transitions from shine position to two-hands joined position, and back to shine position.

Repeat with slow cha-cha music. All transitions in the forward and backward cha-cha motions should occur naturally.

Success Goals = 6 smooth transitions alternating the shine position and the two-hands joined position (a) without music, then (b) with music

Your Score =

a. (#) _____ smoothly alternated transitions (without music)

b. (#) _____ smoothly alternated transitions (with music)

4. Cha-Cha Sideward Leads

Start in a two-hands joined position with your partner (see Figure a). Without doing the cha-cha basic, the man leads sideward by bringing his left hand across the midline of his body and releasing his right-hand grasp. These actions rotate both partners to face the man's right side (inside hands stay joined). Now reverse to face the man's left side: The man brings his left hand back, grasps his partner's left hand with his right hand, releases his left-hand grasp, and continues to bring his right hand across his midline to face his left side (inside hands stay joined).

Without music, do four cha-cha basics forward and backward. On the fourth cha-cha (see Figure b), the man releases his right-hand grasp (on Counts 1, 2) and brings his left hand across his midline (on Counts 3-and-4). Both partners end up facing the man's right side. Do the next Counts 1, 2, with inside feet (see Figure c). The man rotates CCW to face his partner and grasp both of her hands (see Figure d) during Counts 3-and-4 (as both travel sideward). The man releases his left-hand grasp, brings his right hand across his midline to face his left side (see Figure e). Both do the next Counts 1, 2, with inside feet (see Figure f). The man rotates CW to face his partner and grasp both of her hands (see Figure g) during the next Counts 3-and-4 (moving sideward).

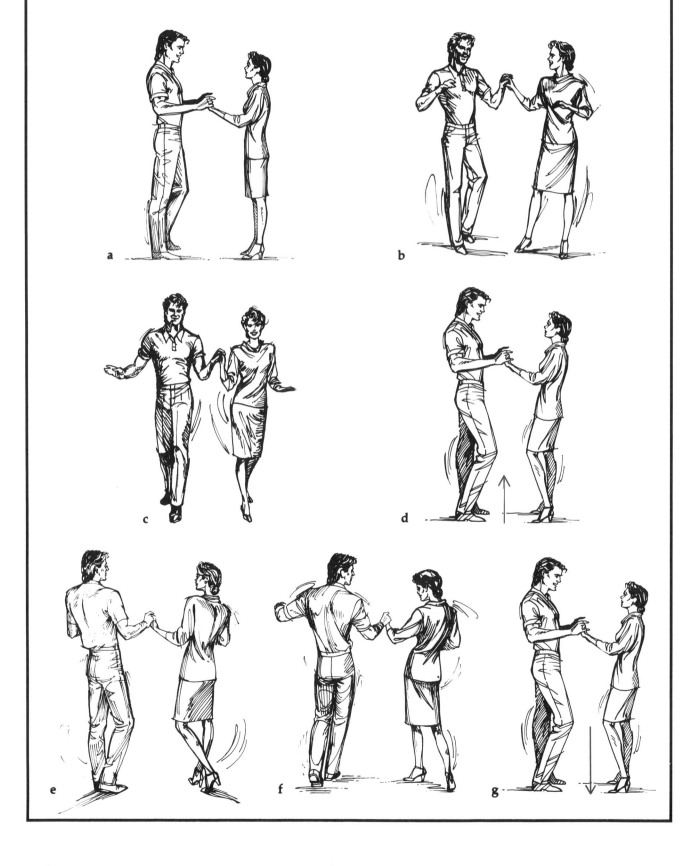

With music, repeat the cha-cha sideward leads. The leads need to be given early enough that the woman can respond appropriately. To summarize, both partners' shoulders face to the man's right side, parallel, face to the man's left side, then parallel. Do at least six consecutive sideward cha-cha basics. Notice that your cha-cha-cha steps now move directly sideward (more like a side step, close, side step).

Success Goals = 6 correctly timed sideward leads from a two-hands joined position with 6 consecutive sideward cha-cha basics (a) without music, then (b) with music

Your Score =

a. (#) ____ correctly timed sideward leads with (#) ____ consecutive sideward basics (without music)

b. (#) ____ correctly timed sideward leads with (#) ____ consecutive sideward basics (with music)

5. *Combining Four Cha-Cha Directional Leads*

Before blending all these directions together, you need to know how to get from the sideward leads back to the forward and backward leads. Walk through the previous drill and freeze before the fourth cha-cha-cha sideward steps (to the man's right). The man holds onto both of his partner's hands and gently pushes his left hand and arm forward—as both partners continue moving sideward! This indicates to the woman that the next cha-cha basic is to be done forward and backward.

Without music, practice at least six transitions on the fourth sideward cha-cha basic to correctly lead your partner back into the forward and backward cha-cha basic.

Establish a short combination to music by blending the four cha-cha directional leads as follows:

• Start in a shine position, and move forward and backward.
• Move closer into a two-hands joined position.
• On any backward half of the cha-cha basic, the man can release his right hand, then bring his left hand across his midline during the cha-cha-cha steps.

- Do four basic cha-cha steps to the man's right, left, right, and left sides.
- On any left side, the man can press his left hand forward during the sideward cha-cha-cha steps.
- Move forward and backward in a two-hands joined position.
- Release hands to return to a shine position.

Success Goals =

a. 6 correctly timed transitions from a sideward to a forward and backward direction (without music)

b. 4 successful repetitions of the previous combinations (blending four directional changes) to music

Your Score =

a. (#) ____ correctly timed transitions from a sideward to a forward and backward direction (without music)

b. (#) ____ successful repetitions of the four-direction combination to music

(Cha-cha variations and combination options continue in Step 8.)

Drills for Waltz Leads, Transitions, and Short Combinations

1. Forward and Backward Waltz Leads

With a partner, stand in a closed dance position (see Figure 6.1, d and e). Once you are in a closed dance position, your hands, arms, shoulders, and torso need to form a semirigid frame. Therefore, when the man moves his body weight forward over the balls of his feet and off his heels, both partners' entire bodies should move in the intended direction (i.e., forward for the man). Check that neither partner's elbows bend or change their original curved shapes. Maintaining a proper frame puts limits on the space that your partner can enter, which facilitates both leading and following. Can you both feel this forward lead?

Now the man can signal his partner to move backward (from the man's point of view, because the woman actually moves toward her partner). The man transfers his body weight toward his heels as he keeps his entire frame, and especially his right hand and open palm, firm. The woman should feel the man's hand pressure just below her left shoulder blade, which signals her to move toward the man. Can you both feel this backward lead?

Do eight alternating forward and backward leads.

Success Goal = 8 alternating forward and backward leads correctly executed with a partner in a closed dance position and with a proper frame

Your Score = (#) ____ alternating forward and backward leads correctly executed with a partner in a closed dance position and with a proper frame

2. Waltz Box-Step Leads

To lead the forward half of a box step with your partner, begin in a closed dance position. Mentally count in threes to get the tempo of the music. Prior to any Count 1, the man transfers his body weight forward as previously done, and also *slightly* lifts his right elbow (no more than 2 inches). This signals to his partner that they are going to execute a forward half-box: forward, side, close (the woman's footwork is the reverse: backward, side, close).

To lead the backward half of a box step, the man keeps his right hand firm on his partner's back and lightly pulls his right hand and entire frame backward at the end of Count 3. This action needs to be timed with the subtle "falling" action characteristic of the waltz (i.e., a lowering of weight before the long reach step). Then complete the backward half-box. Work for a fluid connection between your steps and the lead actions as you do both halves with your partner at least 16 times. Double-check that your arms and shoulders are in their correct closed dance positions throughout your box steps.

Success Goal =   16 fluid repetitions of the full box step with proper leads to music

Your Score =   (#) _____ fluid repetitions of the full box step with proper leads to music

3. Left Box-Turn Lead

The left box turn is composed of four CCW quarter turns. To lead into the left box turn, the man must rotate his entire upper torso (keeping his frame firm) in isolation from his lower torso. This action is similar to turning a steering wheel, except that the center of your body is part of the wheel (more than just your arms turn). Experiment with a few twists of your upper torso with your partner from a stationary position.

There are two directions that are alternately used in the left box turn: the left diagonal front, and the right diagonal back. Both directions are dependent upon where your midline is facing (which alternately changes as you make each quarter turn CCW).

Prior to any Count 1, the man begins to twist his upper torso CCW. On Count 1, the man's left foot toes out 90 degrees, and the woman's right foot toes in 90 degrees, while both step on a 45-degree diagonal (the man's left front; and the woman's right back). The quarter turn is accomplished on Count 1, then Counts 2 and 3 are taken to the side and together.

For the second half-box, the man continues to rotate his upper torso CCW. Now, on Count 1, the man's right foot toes in 90 degrees, and the woman's left foot toes out 90 degrees, while both step on a 45-degree diagonal (the man's right back, and the woman's left front). Again, the quarter turn is accomplished on Count 1, and Counts 2 and 3 are taken to the side and together (180 degrees from the O.F.).

The third and fourth half-box steps repeat the above. To end the turn, the man firmly keeps his upper torso facing his O.F. Do at least four left box turns, first without music and then with slow waltz music.

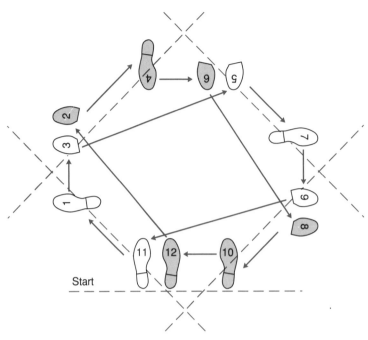

a   Man's left box turn

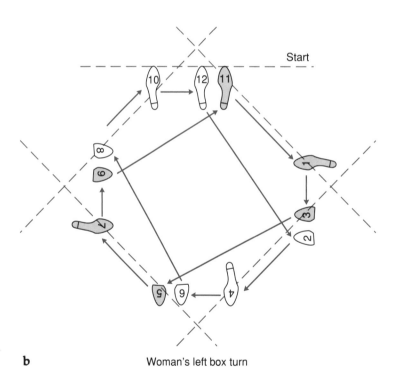

b   Woman's left box turn

Success Goals = 4 waltz left box turns in correct position and with proper leads (a) without music, then (b) with music

Your Score =

   a. (#) _____ waltz left box turns in correct position and with proper leads (without music)

   b. (#) _____ waltz left box turns in correct position and with proper leads (with music)

4. Waltz Half-Box Progression Forward

The half-box step can be done forward in an alternating manner, called the half-box progression forward. The lead for this variation begins exactly as for the waltz box step, and then a new lead needs to signal continued forward motion. Thus, on Count 3 the man should continue leaning forward (from his heels, not his waist). The timing of this lead is critical, because if the man hesitates even slightly, the woman will think that the man wants to do the waltz box step.

The man's footwork action alternates starting forward with his left foot (for one half of a waltz box step), then forward with his right foot (for one half of a waltz box step). The woman does the same alternating footwork but starts with her right foot and travels backward.

Do at least eight consecutive repetitions of the half-box progression forward without music. As you travel CCW around the perimeter of the room, follow a straight path along the length of the room, and follow a curved path along the width of the room.

Repeat these movements to slow waltz music.

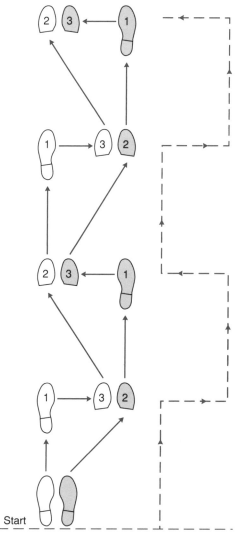

a   Man's half-box progression forward

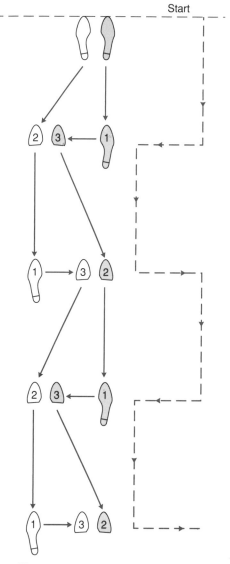

b   Woman's half-box progression forward

Success Goals = 8 consecutive repetitions of half-box waltz progressions forward, properly led, (a) without music, then (b) with music

Your Score =

a. (#) ___ consecutive half-box waltz progressions forward, properly led, without music

b. (#) ___ consecutive half-box waltz progressions forward, properly led, with music

5. Waltz Half-Box Progression Backward

There is also a backward variation of the half-box progression that reverses the footwork used in the forward variation. The man transfers his weight backward and pulls his right hand toward himself (back) as he starts the half-box backward with his left foot. He repeats this weight transfer and right-hand pull on Count 3, and continues the next half-box backward with his right foot. Do at least four half-box progressions backward without music. Again, check that your timing before the second half-box progression backward is clear to the woman. Any hesitation signals a waltz box step.

Then practice the half-box progression backward variation in the following order:

- Four half-box progression forward steps
- Four half-box progression backward steps

Be aware that this particular practice combination is not appropriate for traveling in the LOD at this point. However, later you will be able to travel when you know more variations and options (these are presented in Step 11). Remember to move in unison with your partner to create a fluid, ongoing sequence.

Success Goals = 8 consecutive combinations of alternating 4 forward and 4 backward half-box waltz progressions, properly led, (a) without music, then (b) with music

Your Score =

a. (#) ___ consecutive combinations of alternating 4 forward and 4 backward half-box waltz progressions, properly led, without music

b. (#) ___ consecutive combinations of alternating 4 forward and 4 backward half-box waltz progressions, properly led, with music

6. Combining Two Waltz Variations

Using the appropriate waltz leads with your partner, do each of the following combinations at least eight times to slow waltz music:

- Two boxes and a left box turn
- Two boxes and four half-box progressions forward
- Four half-box progressions forward and a left box turn

Now create a continuous waltz sequence to travel in the LOD with music. Repeat as many half-box progressions forward as necessary to travel the length of the room, then do one quarter-turn left (to turn the corner), repeat as many half-box progressions forward (now starting with the man's right foot) as necessary to travel the width of the room, then do one quarter-turn left (to turn the next corner), and continue the half-box progressions forward (starting with the man's right foot) until you and your partner have traveled twice around the perimeter of the room (LOD).

Success Goals =

a. 8 consecutive repetitions of each of the listed waltz combinations, properly led to slow waltz music

b. 2 consecutive circles in the LOD using proper leads, to slow waltz music, alternating multiple half-box progressions forward (to maintain forward motion for the length of the room) and 1 quarter-turn left (to turn the corner)

Your Score =

a. (#) _____ consecutive repetitions of alternating 2 boxes and a left box turn

(#) _____ consecutive repetitions of alternating 2 boxes and 4 half-box progressions forward

(#) _____ consecutive repetitions of alternating 4 half-box progressions forward and a left box turn

b. (#) _____ consecutive circles in the LOD using half-box progressions forward and a left quarter turn.

(Waltz variations and combination options continue in Step 11.)

Drills for Polka Leads, Transitions, and Short Combinations

1. Swinging Inside Hands Lead

Stand beside a partner (with the woman on the right and the man on the left). Partners extend inside hands and join them (review Figure 6.1, g and h). Place your outside hands on your hips and keep them there whenever they are free. Travel down and back the length of the room during each of the following drill parts.

a. Do at least eight polka basics with your partner, with inside hands joined. Each of you should hop on your inside foot, and step with your outside foot (into the triple step), then hop on your outside foot, and step with your inside foot (into the triple step). Or, you can start the triple step with your outside foot on the downbeat and add the hop on the "and" count prior to the next triple step. After you get started, both methods place the hop on the upbeat.

b. You might have noticed a natural tendency to let your inside hands and arms swing forward and backward as you and your partner practiced the polka. This arm-swinging motion adds style to your polka. Exaggerate this natural swinging motion of your inside hands and arms by doing the following: Gently bring your inside hands back, and notice what happens to your upper torso. This should rotate you to face your partner (front to front). Then gently bring your inside hands forward, and notice what happens to your upper torso. This should rotate your shoulders away from your partner (back to back).

Without music, do at least eight polka basics with your inside hands and arms swinging back with the first polka basic (see Figure a), then forward for the next polka basic (see Figure b). These arm swings should move freely without a lot of force or effort. Avoid overtwisting, as your toes should still point forward during the polka basics.

c. Repeat part b to slow polka music. Make sure that a natural (rather than forced) arm swing occurs with each polka basic.

a

b

Success Goals =

a. 8 consecutive polka basics forward from an inside-hands joined position (without music)

b. 8 consecutive polka basics forward from an inside-hands joined position with a natural arm swing occurring with each polka basic (without music)

c. 8 consecutive polka basics forward from an inside-hands joined position with a natural arm swing occurring with each polka basic (with music)

Your Score =

a. (#) _____ consecutive polka basics in correct position and without swinging arms (without music)

b. (#) _____ consecutive polka basics in correct position with a natural arm swing occurring with each polka basic (without music)

c. (#) _____ consecutive polka basics in correct position with a natural arm swing occurring with each polka basic (with music)

2. Travel in LOD

Repeat part c of the previous drill, except continue moving forward in the LOD to make a circular path around the perimeter of the room. Stay on the outside edge as you travel in the LOD. Travel at least twice around the room. Slowly angle yourself and your partner to gradually rotate CCW to travel in a curved path at the ends of the room. Continue to freely swing inside arms with each polka basic (arms swing back with outside feet, then forward with inside feet).

Success Goal = 2 circular paths traveled in the LOD to slow polka music

Your Score = (#) _____ circular paths traveled in the LOD to slow polka music

3. Semiopen-Position Lead Forward

Stand beside your partner (woman on right, man on left), and position yourselves in a semi-open position (see Figure 6.1f). Keep this semiopen position, and do continuous polka basics while moving in the LOD to slow polka music. Part of the proper lead is to maintain a firm, extended outside arm (not letting the arms move up and down).

Success Goal = 16 continuous polka basics in semiopen position with a firm frame

Your Score = (#) _____ continuous polka basics in semiopen position with a firm frame

4. Transition Lead Into the Semiopen Position

If you start the polka basics from an inside-hands joined position, how do you lead into the semiopen position?

Technically, any time your inside hands and arms swing back (and you step with your outside foot), the man can begin the lead for this transition. For example, take two polka basics with a partner and let inside arms swing back and forward. On your third polka basic, swing back as usual (see Figure a), but the man places the woman's hand on top of his right shoulder (see Figures b and c). On the fourth polka basic, the man releases his right hand, places it just below the woman's left shoulder blade (see Figure d), and extends his outside (left) arm and hand forward so that the woman can put her right hand on top (see Figure e). Do four polka basics in semiopen position. Practice this transition lead with your partner at least four times without music.

Repeat this sequence of eight polka basics at least eight times to slow polka music.

Success Goals =

a. 4 correct transitions from an inside-hands joined position to a semiopen position (without music)

b. 8 correct transitions from an inside-hands joined position to a semiopen position (with music)

Your Score =

a. (#) _____ correct transitions (without music)

b. (#) _____ correct transitions (with music)

5. *Transition Lead From a Semiopen Position to an Inside-Hands Joined Position*

If you start doing polka basics from a semiopen position (see Figure a), how do you lead into the inside-hands joined position?

Any time the outside feet are doing the basic step, the man may give the following leads, which require two polka basics to complete: Release your left hand grasp, slide your right hand to the woman's left side, and gently press with the heel of your right hand (see Figure b). This slightly pushes the woman away; then slide arms until you both grasp inside hands (see Figure c). Both partners place their outside hands on their hips, and swing inside hands back (see Figure d).

a b

c d

Do four consecutive polka basics in a semiopen position, and then do at least two basics to push away and slide arms back into the inside-hands joined position. Repeat this transition four times.

Repeat this transition at least eight times to slow polka music.

Success Goals =

 a. 4 correct transitions from a semiopen position to an inside-hands joined position (without music)

 b. 8 correct transitions from a semiopen position to an inside-hands joined position (with music)

Your Score =

 a. (#) _____ correct transitions (without music)

 b. (#) _____ correct transitions (with music)

6. Combining Two Transitional Leads

Blend both of the two previous drills together to create a continuous sequence of polka basics. Start from an inside-hands joined position, and do four polka basics with a correct transition into the semiopen position. Do four polka basics from the semiopen position with a correct transition back into an inside-hands joined position. Repeat this sequence at least four times without music, then at least eight times with slow polka music. Travel in the LOD.

Success Goals =

   a. 4 consecutive repetitions combining 2 transitional polka leads (without music)

   b. 8 consecutive repetitions combining 2 transitional polka leads (with music)

Your Score =

   a. (#) ____ consecutive repetitions combining 2 transitional polka leads (without music)

   b. (#) ____ consecutive repetitions combining 2 transitional polka leads (with music)

(Polka variations and combination options continue in Step 10.)

Drills for Fox-Trot Leads, Transitions, and Short Combinations

1. Fox-Trot Box-Step Leads

To lead the forward half of a fox-trot box step with your partner, begin in a closed dance position (see Figure 6.1, d and e). Mentally count in groups of four counts to get the tempo. Prior to any Count 1, the man transfers his body weight forward onto the balls of his feet and slightly lifts his right elbow. Both partners' elbows must lightly touch, for the woman to notice this subtle lead. If both partners' frames are firm, then these actions signal the man's forward direction. Both partners do one half of a fox-trot box step: forward, touch, side, close (starting with man's left foot and woman's right foot).

On Count 2, remember to briefly touch the ball of your free foot beside your stationary foot, and move it directly sideways into the side step. The man should keep his right hand firm below the woman's left shoulder blade and pull with his right-hand fingers to the side before the side step (on Count 3). Then, on Count 4, the man gently pulls his entire right hand toward himself, which signals the woman to follow as the man steps back with his right foot on the next Count 1. Both continue the man's backward half of the box step: backward, touch, side, close (starting with man's right foot and woman's left foot).

Do the entire fox-trot box step at least eight times without music. Then repeat it at least 16 times to slow fox-trot music.

Success Goals =

   a. 8 repetitions of the fox-trot box step in correct position and with proper leads (without music)

   b. 16 repetitions of the fox-trot box step in correct position and with proper leads (with music)

Your Score =

a. (#) ____ repetitions of the fox-trot box step in correct position and with proper leads (without music)

b. (#) ____ repetitions of the fox-trot box step in correct position and with proper leads (with music)

2. *Left Box-Turn Lead*

Start in closed dance position with a partner. To initiate a fox-trot box turn (four CCW quarter turns), the man must twist his upper torso while keeping his chest and shoulders firmly connected to his arms (creating a frame) before any Count 1. This upper torso rotation facilitates both the man's toes-out placement of his left foot and the woman's toes-in placement of her right foot along a 45-degree angle (the man's left front diagonal, and the woman's right back diagonal). Finish the rest of your half-box footwork while facing the first quarter-turn direction.

For the second quarter-turn, the man should again rotate his upper torso CCW just prior to Count 1. This lets the man step along a backward diagonal path with his right foot. Be careful to avoid a tendency to rotate too far—turn only 45 degrees. The woman steps along a forward diagonal path with her left foot. Both partners make the quarter turn with this first step of the half box. Then the remaining "touch, side, close" actions follow.

Repeat the previous actions for the next two quarter-turns. Once back to the original front (after four quarter-turns), the man firmly keeps his upper torso in the closed dance position (avoiding any momentum tendencies to continue the CCW rotation).

Without music, do at least four fox-trot left box turns with the proper upper torso leads. Stop briefly after each left box turn to avoid getting dizzy.

With music, repeat the fox-trot left box turns, making sure that your closed dance position is maintained properly throughout.

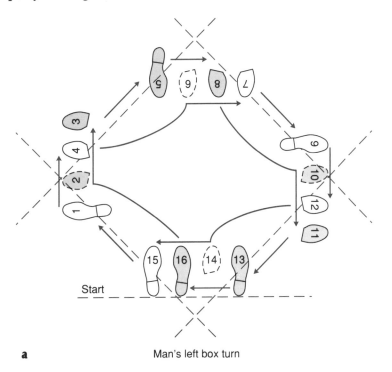

a   Man's left box turn

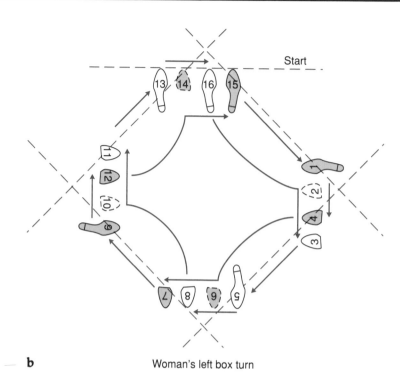

b   Woman's left box turn

Success Goals = 4 fox-trot left box turns in correct position and with proper leads (a) without music, then (b) with music

Your Score =

a. (#) _____ fox-trot left box turns in correct position and with proper leads (without music)

b. (#) _____ fox-trot left box turns in correct position and with proper leads (with music)

3. Magic Step Leads

The magic step was described previously in Step 4 (see Figure 4.4). To lead the magic step with a partner in a closed dance position, the man needs to transfer his weight forward before Count 3, as if he were being pulled by a rope. If the man hesitates even slightly before Count 3, the woman will interpret it to mean that the man wants to do the box step. Make sure that Counts 1 and 2 and Counts 3 and 4 correspond to the man's "forward, forward" reaching steps. Counts 5 and 6 are the "side, close" steps. Make sure that your side steps are taken to the side rather than moving forward.

Do the magic step at least eight times without music, then add music. Travel in the LOD with a partner. How many magic steps can you do consecutively? Notice that too many consecutive magic steps moves both you and your partner closer to the center of the room. Thus, later you will need to alternate the magic step with other fox-trot steps to maintain travel in the LOD.

Success Goals = 8 repetitions of the magic step in correct position and with proper leads (a) without music, then (b) with music

Your Score =

a. (#) _____ repetitions of the magic step in correct position and with proper leads (without music)

b. (#) _____ repetitions of the magic step in correct position and with proper leads (with music)

4. Fox-Trot Half-Box Progressions Forward

Start in a closed dance position with a partner. To lead the fox-trot half-box progression forward, the man transfers his weight forward and slightly lifts his right elbow before any Count 1. Then both partners do a forward, touch, side, close (man starts with the left foot; woman starts with right foot to do the reverse movement). This is the same lead that was used with the forward half of the fox-trot box step.

A new lead is needed for the next half-box, which continues forward. Thus, before the next Count 1, the man must transfer his weight forward. This signals the woman to continue moving in the LOD (forward, for the man). Then complete another half-box forward: The man begins with his right foot; the woman begins with her left foot.

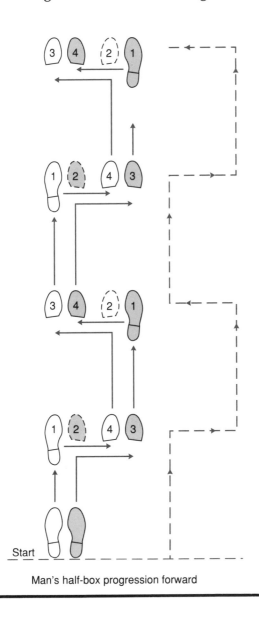

a
Man's half-box progression forward

b
Woman's half-box progression forward

Do at least eight half-box progressions forward without music. Then do at least 16 half-box progressions forward with fox-trot music. Travel along a curved path at the ends of the room.

Success Goals =

a. 8 fox-trot half-box progressions forward in correct position and with proper leads (without music)

b. 16 fox-trot half-box progressions forward in correct position and with proper leads (with music)

Your Score =

a. (#) _____ fox-trot half-box progressions forward in correct position and with proper leads (without music)

b. (#) _____ fox-trot half-box progressions forward in correct position and with proper leads (with music)

5. Fox-Trot Half-Box Progressions Backward

The fox-trot half-box progression can be executed backward as well as forward. Start in a closed dance position with a partner. To lead backward, the man gently pulls his right hand back (toward himself) prior to any Count 1. This signals both partners to reach, touch, side, and close (starting with the man's left foot and the woman's right foot). On the fourth count, the man repeats his gentle pull back to indicate that he wants to continue into another half-box backward. These movements "progress" both partners backward.

A nice practice combination to do is four half-box progressions forward, then four half-box progressions backward. Note that this practice combination is not appropriate for the dance floor until it is modified (see Step 9) to permit you and your partner to travel in the LOD. But it is very helpful at this point to get the idea of the proper timing for your leads—and to incorporate the proper styling of the fox-trot.

Do at least eight repetitions of this combined forward and backward sequence without music, then with music.

Success Goals =   8 repetitions of the combined sequence (4 half-box progressions forward and 4 half-box progressions backward) with correct position and with proper leads (a) without music, then (b) with music

Your Score =

a. (#) _____ repetitions of the combined sequence with correct position and with proper leads, without music

b. (#) _____ repetitions of the combined sequence with correct position and with proper leads, with music

6. Combining Two Fox-Trot Variations

Once a lead is given for a particular step variation, the man should repeat it at least twice before giving a new lead. This gives the man time to plan ahead and the woman time to adjust to the previous leads.

Start in a closed dance position. Using the appropriate fox-trot leads with your partner, do each of the following combinations in the LOD to slow fox-trot music:

- Two boxes and a left box turn
- Two boxes and four half-box progressions forward
- Four half-box progressions forward and a left box turn
- Two boxes and two magic steps
- Four half-box progressions forward and four magic steps

Now create a CCW traveling sequence using as many half-box progressions forward as necessary to travel the length of the room. Then do a quarter turn left (to turn the corner), repeat as many half-box progressions forward (now starting with the man's right foot) as necessary to travel the width of the room, then do a quarter turn left (to turn the next corner), and continue the half-box progressions forward (starting with the man's right foot).

Success Goals =

a. 8 consecutive repetitions of each of the listed fox-trot combinations, in correct position and with proper leads, to slow fox-trot music

b. 2 consecutive circles in the LOD, in correct position and with proper leads for the half-box progressions (for length of the room) and 1 quarter-turn (to turn the corner), to fox-trot music

Your Score =

a. (#) _____ consecutive repetitions of the alternating box and left box-turn combination

(#) _____ consecutive repetitions of the alternating box and half-box progressions forward combination

(#) _____ consecutive repetitions of the alternating half-box progressions forward and left box-turn combination

(#) _____ consecutive repetitions of the alternating box and magic step combination

(#) _____ consecutive repetitions of the alternating half-box progressions forward and magic step combination

b. (#) _____ consecutive circles in the LOD using half-box progressions forward and a left quarter turn

(Fox-trot variations and combination options continue in Step 9.)

Drills for Swing Leads, Transitions, and Short Combinations

All of the leads and transitions for the swing are appropriate for all three swing basic steps: triple lindy (slow tempo), double lindy (moderate tempo), and single lindy (fast tempo). There are two strategies for practicing the swing basic leads. To give you and your partner more time for decision making, one strategy is to do only the triple-lindy basic the first time through all of the following drills. Then you can easily repeat these drills twice with increasingly faster tempos, using the double-lindy basic and finally the single-lindy basic. A second strategy is to challenge yourself by meeting the Success Goals for all three swing basics the first time through each drill. The choice is yours.

1. In-Place Leads

Begin in a semiopen position with a partner. To lead the swing basic in place, the man drops his outside shoulder before any Count 1. This action slightly lowers his left arm and hand as his right elbow slightly lifts. Both partners do the forward half of the swing basic in this position (see Figure a). Prior to Count 3, the man drops his inside shoulder. This action slightly lowers his right arm as his left arm and hand slightly lift. Both partners do the backward half of the swing basic in this position (see Figure b). Prior to Count 5, the man brings his shoulders into the semiopen position again. Both partners' upper bodies remain upright during the ball-change steps (see Figure c).

Do at least eight consecutive swing basics without music, then repeat with the appropriate music tempo.

Success Goals =

a. 8 consecutive swing basics in correct position with proper leads (without music) for each of the following: triple lindy, double lindy, and single lindy

b. 8 consecutive swing basics in correct position with proper leads (with appropriate music tempo) for each of the following: triple lindy (slow), double lindy (moderate), and single lindy (fast)

Your Score =

a. (#) ____ consecutive triple-lindy basics (without music)

(#) ____ consecutive double-lindy basics (without music)

a

b

c

(#) ____ consecutive single-lindy basics
(without music)

b. (#) ____ consecutive triple-lindy basics
(with slow tempo)

(#) ____ consecutive double-lindy
basics (with moderate tempo)

(#) ____ consecutive single-lindy basics
(with fast tempo)

2. CW Rotation Leads

To lead into a CW rotation within your spot, repeat the leads for a forward triple step and
a backward triple step (see the previous drill). Then rotate (twist from the waist) your shoulders
and extended hands one eighth of a turn CW. Do the ball-change portion of your basic step
facing the man's diagonal right front. Stay facing this new direction, and repeat the forward
half and backward half of your basic. Again rotate shoulders and extended hands one eighth
of a turn CW. Now the ball-change portion is done facing the man's original right side. Continue making these slight angle shifts until you get back to your original front (this requires
eight basic steps)—much like turning a steering wheel. Do the CW rotation (eight basics per
rotation) leads at least twice without music, adding any number of in-place basics between
each 360-degrees of rotation.

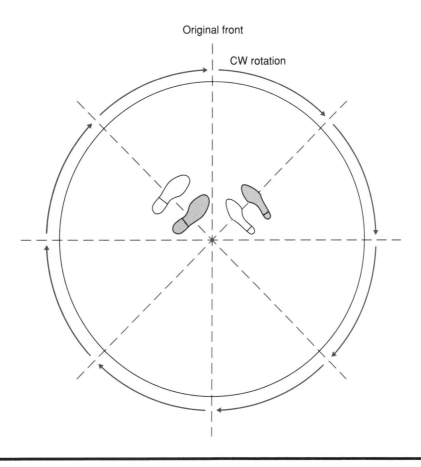

These directional leads may feel mechanical at first. To improve the smoothness (fluidity) of your continuous basic steps, experiment with moving CW throughout: on the forward, on the backward, and on the ball-change steps—so that you both travel and rotate (more than 45 degrees with each basic) at the same time. Stay within your large circle as you travel. Feel free to add any number of in-place basic steps between your rotational changes, but now do less than eight basics per rotation with the appropriate music tempo.

Success Goals =

a. 2 CW rotations of swing basics (8 basics per rotation) in semiopen position with proper leads (without music) for each of the following: triple lindy, double lindy, and single lindy

b. 2 CW rotations of swing basics (less than 8 basics per rotation) in semiopen position with proper leads (with appropriate music tempo) for each of the following: triple lindy (slow), double lindy (moderate), and single lindy (fast)

Your Score =

a. (#) _____ CW rotations using triple-lindy basics (without music)

(#) _____ CW rotations using double-lindy basics (without music)

(#) _____ CW rotations using single-lindy basics (without music)

b. (#) _____ CW rotations using triple-lindy basics (with slow tempo)

(#) _____ CW rotations using double-lindy basics (with moderate tempo)

(#) _____ CW rotations using single-lindy basics (with fast tempo)

3. CCW Rotation Leads

Repeat the previous drill, except rotate CCW. Before the ball-change portion of the basic step, the man twists his shoulders and extended hand CCW one eighth of a 360-degree rotation. Do eight basics to make a full 360-degree CCW rotation with your partner without music. Use any number of in-place basics between each 360-degree rotation to keep from getting dizzy.

Then repeat the CCW rotation with the appropriate music tempo. Work for fluid movements throughout by traveling and rotating more than 45 degrees with each basic.

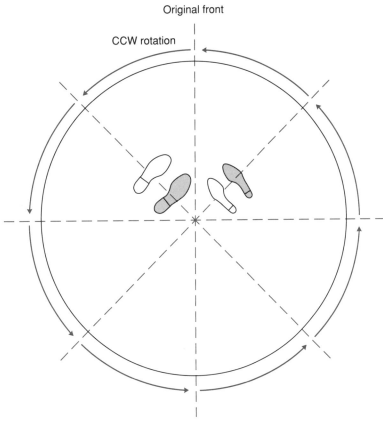

Success Goals =

a. 2 CCW rotations of swing basics (8 basics per rotation) in semiopen position with proper leads (without music) for each of the following: triple lindy, double lindy, and single lindy

b. 2 CCW rotations of swing basics (less than 8 basics per rotation) in semiopen position with proper leads (with appropriate music tempo) for each of the following: triple lindy (slow), double lindy (moderate), and single lindy (fast)

Your Score =

a. (#) _____ CCW rotations using triple-lindy basics (without music)

   (#) _____ CCW rotations using double-lindy basics (without music)

   (#) _____ CCW rotations using single-lindy basics (without music)

b. (#) _____ CCW rotations using triple-lindy basics (with slow tempo)

   (#) _____ CCW rotations using double-lindy basics (with moderate tempo)

   (#) _____ CCW rotations using single-lindy basics (with fast tempo)

4. Arch-Out and Arch-In Transition Leads

The arch-out lead is a transition from the semiopen position out to a one-hand joined position (with the man's left hand and the woman's right hand joined). The arch-in lead is a transition from a one-hand joined position into the semiopen position. Both transitions are done while rotating either CW or CCW with your partner (see Figure a).

To lead the arch-out, begin in a semiopen position with a partner, and repeat the appropriate swing basic at least twice (see Figure b). Then, at the end of any ball-change portion, the man lifts his outside arm, bringing both partners' outside arms up to form an arch (see Figures c and d). This indicates that a turn (an arch-out) for the woman is coming during the *next* basic step. Both partners do the forward half of their basic while the woman moves forward under the arch. On Count 2, the man presses with the heel of his right hand to guide the woman's CW 180-degree turn on her outside foot. Both partners continue their backward half of the basic while facing each other in a one-hand joined position (see Figure e). On Count 5, both partners pull their elbows and hands back (as if pulling on a rein). On Count 6, the man brings his left hand across his midline to his right side, lifting it high into an arch again. This is the lead for the arch-in transition (see Figure f). It indicates that a turn (an arch-in) for the woman is coming during the *next* basic step.

On Count 1 of the arch-in transition, the man pulls his left hand toward himself and lifts both partners' hands above the woman's head. These actions guide the woman forward under the arch as both do the forward half of the basic (see Figure g). On Count 2, the man circles his left hand CCW above the woman's head to lead the woman into a CCW 180-degree turn. Both partners do the backward half of the basic, and the ball-change in the semiopen position (see Figure h).

g   h

From a semiopen position, do two basics in place, then do an arch-out (one basic) into a one-hand joined position, and immediately follow with an arch-in (one basic) into a semi-open position. Repeat this combination at least eight times without music. Then repeat this combination at least 16 times with the appropriate music tempo.

Success Goals =

a. 8 consecutive repetitions of the in-place, arch-out, and arch-in combination in correct position, with proper leads, and without music, for each of the following swing basics: triple lindy, double lindy, and single lindy

b. 16 consecutive repetitions of the in-place, arch-out, and arch-in combination in correct position, with proper leads, and with appropriate music tempo, for each of the following swing basics: triple lindy (slow), double lindy (moderate), and single lindy (fast)

Your Score =

a. (#) _____ consecutive combinations using triple-lindy basics (without music)

 (#) _____ consecutive combinations using double-lindy basics (without music)

 (#) _____ consecutive combinations using single-lindy basics (without music)

b. (#) _____ consecutive combinations using triple-lindy basics (with slow tempo)

 (#) _____ consecutive combinations using double-lindy basics (with moderate tempo)

 (#) _____ consecutive combinations using single-lindy basics (with fast tempo)

5. Roll-Out and Roll-In Transition Leads

The roll-out and the roll-in transitions are alternative ways of moving from a semiopen position to a one-hand joined position and back to a semiopen position again. One major difference in the roll-out and roll-in leads is to keep the hands approximately at waist height rather than lifting them high as in the arch-out and arch-in leads.

To lead the roll-out, begin in a semiopen position with your partner. Both partners repeat the appropriate basic at least twice. At the end of the ball-change portion, the man gently rotates his upper torso CCW to gently lead the woman along a curved path out to the man's left diagonal. Simultaneously, the man pulls with his left arm, pushes with his right hand, and releases his right hand from the woman's back (see Figures a and b). The footwork is the same as for the arch-out transition until the lead on Count 6.

Then, to lead the roll-in, the man gently pulls horizontally inward to lead the woman into the forward half of the basic. On Count 2, the man pulls his left hand in a small horizontal CW circle, which turns the woman 180 degrees (see Figures c and d). Both partners do the backward half of the basic and the ball-change in a semiopen position (see Figure e). Do at least eight roll-out and roll-in transitions without music. Then repeat this combination at least 16 times with the appropriate music tempo.

a

b

c

d

e

Success Goals =

a. 8 consecutive repetitions of the in-place, roll-out, and roll-in combination in correct position, with proper leads, and without music, for each of the following swing basics: triple lindy, double lindy, and single lindy

b. 16 consecutive repetitions of the in-place, roll-out, and roll-in combination in correct position, with proper leads, and with appropriate music tempo, for each of the following swing basics: triple lindy (slow), double lindy (moderate), and single lindy (fast)

Your Score =

a. (#) ____ consecutive combinations using triple-lindy basics (without music)

(#) ____ consecutive combinations using double-lindy basics (without music)

(#) ____ consecutive combinations using single-lindy basics (without music)

b. (#) ____ consecutive combinations using triple-lindy basics (with slow tempo)

(#) ____ consecutive combinations using double-lindy basics (with moderate tempo)

(#) ____ consecutive combinations using single-lindy basics (with fast tempo)

6. Combining Four Leads

Begin in a semiopen position with a partner. Use the appropriate swing basic and music tempo. Review all of the previous swing leads by doing at least two consecutive repetitions of each of the following combinations:

a. In place, CW rotation, arch-out, arch-in
b. In place, CCW rotation, arch-out, arch-in
c. In place, CW rotation, roll-out, roll-in
d. In place, CCW rotation, roll-out roll-in
e. In place, CW rotation, in place, CCW rotation
f. In place, CCW rotation, in place, CW rotation
g. In place, arch-out, arch-in, CW rotation
h. In place, arch-out, arch-in, CCW rotation
i. In place, roll-out, roll-in, CW rotation
j. In place, roll-out, roll-in, CCW rotation

During both the arch-out/arch-in and roll-out/roll-in transitions, the smoothest transition occurs when the man also moves slightly CCW to step into his partner's vacated semiopen position, and then returns CW to his original position. Practice with your partner to keep all motions revolving either CW or CCW. Use any number of in-place basic steps. Repeat the above combinations, making sure that you and your partner are in correct positions and using proper styling.

Success Goals =

a. 2 consecutive repetitions of each of the 10 listed combinations, using correct positions, proper leads, and the appropriate swing basic and music tempo

b. 2 consecutive repetitions of each of the 10 listed combinations, using smooth transitions and the appropriate swing basic and music tempo

Your Score =

a. (#) _____ consecutive repetitions for each of the 10 combinations, using triple-lindy basics

   (#) _____ consecutive repetitions for each of the 10 combinations, using double-lindy basics

   (#) _____ consecutive repetitions for each of the 10 combinations, using single-lindy basics

b. (#) _____ consecutive repetitions for each of the 10 combinations, using triple-lindy basics and smooth transitions

   (#) _____ consecutive repetitions for each of the 10 combinations, using double-lindy basics and smooth transitions

   (#) _____ consecutive repetitions for each of the 10 combinations, using single-lindy basics and smooth transitions

(Swing variations and combination options continue in Step 7.)

Communicating With a Partner
Keys to Success Checklist

Imagine that you are at a dance with at least five couples. In a random order, play at least one song for each of the following dance styles (or use Side B of the soundsheet):

- Cha-cha
- Waltz
- Polka
- Fox-trot
- Swing (three tempos)

Practice either politely asking a partner to dance or graciously accepting an invitation to dance. Once you and your partner are on the dance floor, review all of the leads, transitions, and combinations that you know so far for each dance style.

At the end of each song, thank your partner, and the man should escort the woman to the sidelines. Then, either ask or accept the next song with a different partner (if you continue with the same partner, you can imagine that she or he is a new partner). Blend your footwork with the music and add the appropriate styling characteristics for each dance style.

Ask a teacher or trained observer to rate your execution of the basic partner positions according to the checklist items in Figure 6.1 and to give both you and your partner feedback on your abilities to fluidly connect everything into a smooth performance.

Step 7 Swing Variations and Combination Options

You have already practiced some swing leads, transitions, and short combination options in Step 6. You must be able to repeat these without thinking (if you cannot, then review the swing drills in Step 6 before proceeding further). Then you are ready to learn the new swing variations and options presented here, and to create longer combinations or sequences. New options include three variations from a one-hand joined position (single under, double under, and brush), a transition to a two-hands joined position, three variations from a two-hands joined position (wrap and unwrap, row step, and double cross), and combining all swing options into sequences that stay within your spot.

All of the following leads, transitions, and combinations for the swing are appropriate for all three swing basic-step tempos (slow, moderate, and fast). You can complete the Success Goals for each drill using only the triple lindy at first, because a slower tempo gives you more time for decision making. Then you can easily repeat the drills twice with increasingly faster tempos, using the double lindy and then the single lindy. Or you can choose to use all three tempos consecutively with each drill.

Drills for Swing Variations: One-Hand Joined Position

1. Single Under

To execute the single under, assume a one-hand joined position facing your partner. The lead for the single under is the same as for the arch-in transition (see Figure a), except that as the woman comes forward under the arch, the man now exchanges positions with his partner, in a 180-degree switch, by spinning CW on his outside foot on Count 2 (see Figure b). During this turn, the man keeps all his fingers pointing downward, while the woman loosely cups her hand around the man's fingers (maintaining contact without gripping tightly). Both partners continue the triple step backward (and CW), then pull elbows and hands gently back, away from each other, on Count 5 (see Figure c). Throughout, the woman's footwork is no different than that used with the arch-in transition.

    a. Can you do two, three, or four single unders in a row with your partner? Do each of these without music, then with slow music using the triple-lindy basic.

    b. The man has the choice of leading more than one single under in a row or of leading the arch-in. If he wants to do the single under, he switches places with his partner. If he wants to do the arch-in, he stays in his same location. Start in a one-hand joined position. Do each of the following combinations at least two times with your partner to slow music:

- One single under, arch-in
- Two single unders, arch-in
- Three single unders, arch-in
- Four single unders, arch-in

Variation: Repeat this drill using a faster tempo and the appropriate swing basic.

a   b   c

Success Goals =

a. Correctly repeat 2, 3, then 4 single unders in a row, with a partner, to music

b. 2 repetitions of each of the previous single-under and arch-in combinations to music

Your Score =

a. ____ Correctly repeated 2, 3, then 4 single unders in a row, with a partner, to music (yes or no)

b. (#) ____ repetitions of each of the previous single-under and arch-in combinations to music

2. Three-Lead Sequence

Begin in a semiopen position with a partner. Do as many triple-lindy basics to slow music as you want, to get started. Then the man can lead the arch-out, any number of single unders, and the arch-in to return to the semiopen position.

Repeat this three-lead sequence at least eight times.

Variation: Repeat this drill using a faster tempo and the appropriate swing basic.

Success Goal = 8 consecutive repetitions of the 3-lead sequence

Your Score = (#) ____ consecutive repetitions of the 3-lead sequence

3. Double Under

To execute the double under, proceed as if you are doing a single under, except that the man turns CCW under the arched hands and arms during the *second* triple step. The woman's part remains the same whether she is doing the arch-in, single under, or double under. To avoid hitting heads in the middle, make sure that the woman's turn is completed (Counts 1 and 2) *before* the man turns under his left arm (Counts 3 and 4). You both end up reversing positions 180 degrees and facing your partner to pull elbows back on Count 5. Then the next lead is given on Count 6 to repeat the double under. Use the following timing order: woman under, man under, ball-change.

Counts 1 and 2

Counts 3 and 4

  a. Can you do two, three, or four double unders in a row, with your partner, to slow music?
  b. After any number of double unders, the man has at least three options: (1) to immediately do another double under, (2) to do a single under, or (3) to stay in one place to do the arch-in transition to the semiopen position. Do each of the three options with your partner at least four times to slow music.

Variation: Repeat this entire drill using a faster tempo and the appropriate swing basic.

Success Goals =

  a. Correctly execute 2, 3, and 4 double unders in a row, with a partner, to music
  b. 4 repetitions of each of the 3 options after a double under

Your Score =

  a. _____ Correctly executed 2, 3, and 4 double unders in a row, with a partner, to music (yes or no)
  b. (#) _____ repetitions of each of the 3 options after a double under

4. Four-Lead Sequence

Start from a semiopen position. After any number of triple-lindy basics to slow music, the man can lead the following sequence using any number of repetitions of each variation:

- Arch-out
- Double under
- Single under
- Arch-in

Next, try to vary the sequence. For example, you could do the arch-out, two single unders, one double under, and an arch-in. Or you could do the arch-out, one double under, two single unders, and an arch-in.

Variation: Repeat this entire drill using a faster tempo and the appropriate swing basic.

Success Goals =

a. 4 consecutive repetitions of this 4-lead sequence with proper styling, to music

b. Create 3 different sequences that vary either or both the order and the number of repetitions in the previous 4-lead sequence

Your Score =

a. (#) _____ consecutive repetitions of this 4-lead sequence with proper styling to music

b. Sequence 1: _____

   Sequence 2: _____

   Sequence 3: _____

Circle the number of the sequence that flows most easily for you.

5. Half-Rotation Turn

Start in a one-hand joined position with a partner. To lead the half-rotation turn, the man pulls his left hand toward himself (see Figure a), then circles his hand horizontally CW (at a point slightly higher than his waist). Both partners begin to do a triple step forward, then the man's lead rotates both partners 180 degrees CW on Count 2. Both the forward and the backward portions of the triple lindy are executed while moving along a small, CW circle (see Figure b). The regular ball-change follows. This lead is similar to the roll-in transition lead, except the man now turns at the same time as the woman turns.

a

a. Can you do two, three, or four half-rotation turns in a row, with a partner, to slow music?

b. Can you alternately repeat the single under and the half-rotation turn using any number of repeats of each? For example, try alternating two single unders and two half-rotation turns. Or try alternating one single under and one half-rotation turn. How many repetitions of each variation feels best to you—so that you can perform this combination at least eight consecutive times with the music?

c. Can you alternately repeat the double under and the half-rotation turn using any number of repeats of each? How many repetitions of each variation feels best to you—so that you can perform this combination at least eight consecutive times with the music?

b

Variation: Repeat this entire drill using a faster tempo and the appropriate swing basic.

Success Goals =

a. Correctly execute 2, 3, and 4 half-rotation turns in a row, with a partner, to music

b. List the number of repetitions of the single under and the half-rotation turn that works best for you and your partner to continuously repeat to music 8 times

c. List the number of repetitions of the double under and the half-rotation turn that works best for you and your partner to continuously repeat to music 8 times

Your Score =

a. ____ Correctly executed 2, 3, and 4 half-rotation turns in a row, with a partner, to music (yes or no)

b. (#) ____ single under(s) and (#) ____ half-rotation turn(s) work best to continuously repeat to music 8 times

c. (#) ____ double under(s) and (#) ____ half-rotation turn(s) work best to continuously repeat to music 8 times

6. *Five-Lead Sequence*

Begin in a semiopen position with a partner. After any number of triple-lindy basics to slow music, the man can lead the following sequence using any number of repetitions of each:

- Arch-out
- Single under
- Double under
- Half-rotation turn
- Roll-in

a. Repeat this five-lead sequence at least four times. Add the proper swing styling throughout.
b. Repeat this five-lead sequence varying both the order and the number of repetitions of the single under, double under, and half-rotation turn. Can you create at least three different sequences? For example, you could do an arch-out, two single unders, one double under, four half-rotation turns, and a roll-in. Or you could do an arch-out, two double unders, two half-rotation turns, two single unders, and a roll-in. Which sequence works best for you?

Variation: Repeat this entire drill using a faster tempo and the appropriate swing basic.

Success Goals =

a. 4 consecutive repetitions of this 5-lead sequence with proper styling to music
b. Create 3 different sequences that vary either or both the order and the number of repetitions in the previous 5-lead sequence

Your Score =

a. (#) ＿＿ consecutive repetitions of this 5-lead sequence with proper styling to music

b. Sequence 1: ＿＿＿＿＿＿＿＿＿＿＿＿＿＿＿＿＿＿＿＿＿＿＿＿＿＿＿

Sequence 2: ＿＿＿＿＿＿＿＿＿＿＿＿＿＿＿＿＿＿＿＿＿＿＿＿＿＿＿

Sequence 3: ＿＿＿＿＿＿＿＿＿＿＿＿＿＿＿＿＿＿＿＿＿＿＿＿＿＿＿

Circle the number of the sequence that flows most easily.

7. Brush

To execute the brush, the man does the following during Counts 3 and 4 of a basic step: transfers the woman's right hand from his left hand into his right hand (see Figure a). Both partners continue to pull back with right hands and elbows on Count 5. On Count 6, the man rotates his wrist CCW (as if turning a door knob). During the next triple step forward, the man passes the woman on her right (see Figure b). He lowers his hand below his waist and spins CCW on Count 2 as he passes the woman's hand (from his right hand to his left hand) around hip level—keeping elbows curved (not sharply bent) to avoid hitting his partner (see Figure c). The woman does the same footwork used with the half-rotation turn. Then both partners triple step

a

backward and ball-change facing each other (see Figure d).

  a. Try the following with your partner:

- Can you alternately do one basic in place (to transfer the woman's hand on the second triple step) and one brush step at least four times to music?
- Can you alternately repeat a half-rotation turn (to transfer the woman's hand on the second triple step) and a brush step at least four times to music?

  b. You will notice that your hand grip is awkward after the low pass behind your back, because it is the reverse of your normal swing grasp (see Figure d). To get your normal grasp back, you have two immediate variation options—to lead either (1) a single under or (2) a double under. Can you add either a single under or a double under (using any number of repetitions of each) after the brush step? Do at least four repetitions of each combination to music.

Variation: Repeat this entire drill using a faster tempo and the appropriate music.

b

c

Success Goals =

  a. 4 repetitions of alternating 1 swing basic and 1 brush step to music

  b. 4 repetitions of alternating 1 half-rotation turn and 1 brush step to music

  c. 4 repetitions of adding a single under after the brush step to music

  d. 4 repetitions of adding a double under after the brush step to music

Your Score =

  a. (#) ____ repetitions of alternating 1 swing basic and 1 brush step to music

  b. (#) ____ repetitions of alternating 1 half-rotation turn and 1 brush step to music

  c. (#) ____ repetitions of adding a single under after the brush step to music

  d. (#) ____ repetitions of adding a double under after the brush step to music

d

8. Six-Lead Combination

Begin in a semiopen position with a partner. After any number of triple-lindy basics to slow music, the man can lead the following sequence using any number of repetitions of each:

- Arch-out
- Single under
- Double under
- Half-rotation turn
- Brush step
- Repeat a single (or double) under
- Arch-in

a. Repeat this six-lead sequence at least four times. Add the proper swing styling throughout.
b. Repeat this six-lead sequence varying both the order and the number of repetitions of each. Can you create at least three different sequences?

Variation: Repeat this entire drill using a faster tempo and the appropriate swing basic.

Success Goals =

a. 4 consecutive repetitions of this 6-lead sequence with proper styling to music

b. Create 3 different sequences that vary either or both the order and the number of repetitions in the previous 6-lead sequence

Your Score =

a. (#) _____ consecutive repetitions of this 6-lead sequence with proper styling to music

b. Sequence 1: _____

Sequence 2: _____

Sequence 3: _____

Circle the number of the sequence that flows most easily for you.

Drills for Swing Variations: Two-Hands Joined Position

9. Transition to the Two-Hands Joined Position

How do you get into a two-hands joined position? One easy transition is a modification of the half-rotation turn. As the man horizontally circles his left hand to begin the CW rotation with his partner, he also cups his right hand and places it, palm-up, close to the outside of his right hip (see Figure a). This signals the woman to place her hand in his when the half-rotation turn brings her closer to the man (see Figure b).

Be prepared to do more than one half-rotation turn in a row to give the woman an opportunity to place her hand in the man's. The man should avoid reaching out to grab the woman's hand. It is smoother to use the momentum from the CW turn to more naturally connect hands as the turn on Count 2 brings you closer together.

To get out of the two-hands joined position, the man merely lets go with his right hand. Do at least four repetitions of these transitions, both into and out of a two-hands joined position, with a partner to slow music.

Variation: Repeat this drill using a faster tempo and the appropriate swing basic.

a

b

Success Goal = 4 transitions both into and out of a two-hands joined position to music

Your Score = (#) _____ transitions both into and out of a two-hands joined position to music

10. Wrap and Unwrap

The wrap and unwrap basically reverses the order of the arch-out and arch-in transitions— you'll feel like you are doing the arch-in first, and then the arch-out (but with two hands held).

Begin in a two-hands joined position. The man's lead for the wrap is twofold: He brings both hands across his midline to his right side, while keeping his right hand low and to his right; then he lifts his left hand high and CCW above the woman's head (see Figure a). These actions both turn the woman 180 degrees CCW and place her on the man's right side. The woman's footwork is the same as for a single under, except that both hands are held and the woman ends up standing to the right

a

of the man (see Figure b). Both partners do the triple step backward and the ball-change while standing side by side.

To unwrap, the man lifts the outside arms and hands (on Count 6 of any basic step) to form an arch (see Figure c). This signals the woman to turn CW 180 degrees on Count 2 of the *next* basic step forward. Also on Count 2, the man gently presses with the heel of his right hand on his partner's back. As usual, partners face to do the triple step backward and the ball-change. Notice that the man's footwork for the wrap and unwrap is done in place (with no rotation).

b

c

a. Repeat the wrap and unwrap at least four times to music, using one basic for each.
b. Repeat part a, except add two or more basic steps while in the wrap position with your partner.
c. Start in a one-hand joined position with your partner. The man can lead the following combination adding any number of basics between each:

- Half-rotation transition
- Wrap
- Unwrap

Repeat this three-lead sequence, varying the number of basics between each variation, to create at least three different sequences. Use slow music at first.

Variation: Repeat this entire drill with a faster tempo and using the appropriate swing basic.

Success Goals =

a. 4 repetitions of the wrap and unwrap to music

b. 4 repetitions of the wrap, 2 or more basics, and the unwrap to music

c. Create 3 different sequences, varying the number of basics between each, to music

Your Score =

a. (#) _____ repetitions of the wrap and unwrap to music

b. (#) _____ repetitions of the wrap, 2 or more basics, and the unwrap to music

c. Sequence 1: _____

Sequence 2: _____

Sequence 3: _____

11. Row Step

The row step is a fun variation that takes advantage of centrifugal force. Because this step involves spinning first on one foot and then on the other, it is always done with a single-lindy basic, even if you are dancing to slow or moderate tempos. Once the row step is over, resume whatever swing basic step is most appropriate for the music's tempo.

Stand facing your partner, and imagine that there is a small circle between the two of you. Label this circle as a clock (notice that each partner's 12 o'clock is in the direction the partner's midline is facing). Each partner stands at her or his own 6 o'clock, facing a partner positioned at 12 o'clock.

Prior to Count 1, and with partners holding both hands, the man draws an imaginary arrow on an imaginary bow—his left elbow pulls back and his right arm is extended at shoulder height. This lead needs to be a firm action that rotates both partners' shoulders 45 degrees toward their own diagonal left, which brings both partners' right shoulders closer together (see Figure a). On Counts 1 and 2, both partners step forward on the circle at their own 9 o'clocks (the man with his left foot, the woman with her right foot).

On Counts 3 and 4, both partners spin CW 180 degrees (the man with his left foot, the woman with her right foot). During this half turn, the man also reverses his arm positions, so that his left arm is extended and his right elbow is bent, which brings both partners' left shoulders closer to the inside of the circle (see Figure b). In this position, the man brings his right foot behind his left, while the woman brings her feet together.

Then both partners face each other to do the regular ball portion of the basic with the gentle pull back for Count 5 (see Figure c). On Count 6, the man can opt to repeat the row step or go into another variation during the change portion.

Notice that the "bow and arrow" lead for the row step is executed at shoulder height, which distinguishes it from a half-rotation turn (executed at waist height). Both partners need to keep both arms flexible yet firm enough to provide enough resistance for the proper lead. Avoid "spaghetti arms" here! Your arms and shoulders need to act together, so that a gentle push or pull on your hand will cause your entire upper torso (and not just your arms) to rotate.

Use the following cues: "right shoulders in, left shoulders in," and "shoulders square" for the ball-change. Do at least two consecutive row steps with a partner to slow music.

Variation: Repeat this drill using a faster tempo and the appropriate swing basic.

a

Counts 1,2

b

Counts 3,4

c

Counts 5,6

Success Goal = 2 consecutive repetitions of the row step to music

Your Score = (#) ____ consecutive repetitions of the row step to music

12. Double Cross

The double cross can be done alone or immediately after any number of row steps, and it is a transition to get into a modified one-hand joined position—right hand to right hand.

You can do the double cross in 10, 8, or 6 total counts (including the ball-change). Start with the slowest version, then feel free to modify your counts later. Stand facing your partner in a two-hands joined position. There are either no basic steps in the first portion of the double cross, only the following body positions, or one step can be taken within each pivot:

- Face partner: On Counts 1 and 2, the man lifts both arms and hands high to form two arches (see Figure a).
- Pivot left: On Counts 3 and 4, the man pivots CCW as he keeps both hands and arms high to indicate that the woman should pivot CCW also to stand under the arches (see Figure b).
- Stay left: On Counts 5 and 6, while still holding onto his partner's hands, the man places his right hand behind his partner's head and his left hand behind his own head (see Figure c).
- Pivot right: On Counts 7 and 8, the man releases both hands, but both partners keep their inside (right) arms on each other's shoulder as they pivot CW to face each other (see Figure d).
- Slide arms: On the final Counts 9 and 10, slide right hands down each other's arm to grasp hands again during the ball-change portion of your basic step (see Figure e).

Slowly walk through the double cross with a partner, using the following cues: "Lift arms, quarter turn CCW, lower arms, quarter

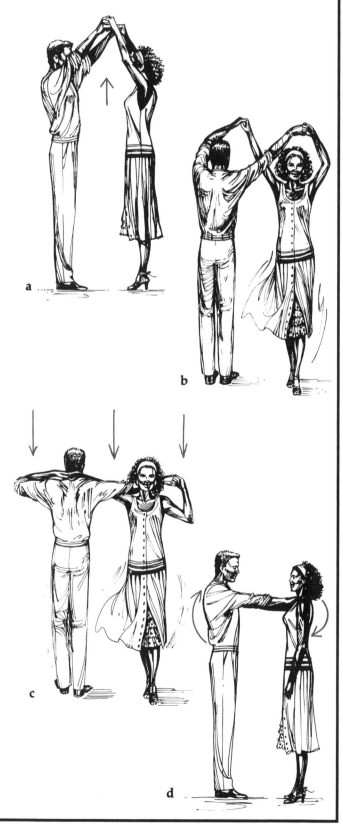

a

b

c

d

turn CW, and slide hands during the ball-change." Try this variation at least four times to music.

Variation: Repeat this drill using a faster tempo and the appropriate swing basic.

Success Goal = 4 repetitions of the double cross with a partner to music

Your Score = (#) _____ repetitions of the double cross with a partner to music

13. *Natural Combinations*

Some variations flow together very well. Start in a two-hands joined position with a partner. Try each of the following combinations to slow music.

a. Do a wrap, two basics, and release with the man's right hand (the woman's left hand) during the unwrap. This is an easy transition into a one-hand joined position. Repeat this transition combination at least four times with fluidity.

b. Do as many repetitions of the row step as you desire, then do a double cross. Repeat this two-lead combination at least four times with fluidity and proper styling.

c. After you finish a double cross, you are in a perfect situation to do a brush—which is typically followed by either a single under or a double under. Do a double cross, a brush, and a single (or double) under. Repeat this three-lead combination at least four times with fluidity and proper styling.

d. Combine both parts b and c to form one long sequence using the following order:

- Row step
- Double cross
- Brush
- Single (or double) under

Repeat this four-lead sequence at least four times with fluidity and proper styling.

Variation: Repeat this entire drill using a faster tempo and the appropriate swing basic.

Success Goals =

a. 4 repetitions of the previous transition combination, fluidly, to music

b. 4 repetitions of the previous 2-lead combination, with fluidity and proper styling, to music

c. 4 repetitions of the previous 3-lead combination, with fluidity and proper styling, to music

d. 4 repetitions of the previous 4-lead combination, with fluidity and proper styling, to music

Your Score =

a. (#) ____ repetitions of transition combination, fluidly, to music

b. (#) ____ repetitions of 2-lead combination, with fluidity and proper styling, to music

c. (#) ____ repetitions of 3-lead combination, with fluidity and proper styling, to music

d. (#) ____ repetitions of 4-lead combination, with fluidity and proper styling, to music

Drill for Swing Combination Options

14. Three-Position Combinations

Create one long swing sequence that includes at least one variation from each of the three positions with appropriate transitions (see the following chart). You can place them in any order and use any number of repetitions of each. Select the variations that you do best, and remember to add styling. Practice your sequence to the tempo of your choice. Repeat your selected sequence three times in a row. Rehearse with your partner until you feel comfortable enough either to imagine that you are performing before an audience or to demonstrate your selected sequence for others to watch.

Variation: Repeat this drill creating three different, spontaneous sequences.

Swing Combination Options Chart

Semiopen Position Variations

1. Basic step
   - In place
   - CW
   - CCW

Two-Hands Joined Position Variations

1. Half-rotation turn
2. Wrap and unwrap
3. Row step
4. Double cross

One-Hand Joined Position Variations

1. Single under
2. Double under
3. Brush
4. Half-rotation turn

Transitions

1. Arch-out and arch-in
2. Roll-out and roll-in
3. Half-rotation transition
4. Release one hand during unwrap

Success Goal = 3 continuous repetitions of your selected sequence with fluidity and styling (to any tempo you prefer)

Your Score = (#) ____ continuous sequence repetitions with fluidity and styling

Step 8 Cha-Cha Variations and Combination Options

Step 6 covered the basic leads and transitions for traveling in four different directions (forward, backward, and to both sides), so you are ready to begin the fun process of experimenting both with selected variations of the basic cha-cha step and with the potential combination options available to you.

Drills for the Cha-Cha Variations: Shine Position

Both of the following variations in the shine position exemplify the "teasing" and flirting with the eyes that are characteristic of the cha-cha, because you continue to look over your shoulder toward your partner as long as you can on each turn. The first variation involves a half turn, and the second variation involves a full turn. Each variation takes four counts.

Both variations involve a follow-the-leader challenge—the man does a variation, and then the woman must repeat that same variation. This alternating process continues until the man stops turning and faces his partner, which nonverbally signals that the "chase" is over.

1. Half Chase

As its name implies, the half chase involves a half turn before the cha-cha-cha portion of the cha-cha basic. First try the half chase without music or a partner. Men and women do exactly the same movements, but at different times. The execution of the half chase *always* occurs on the forward half of the cha-cha basic. As usual, place your left foot forward on Count 1 (see Figure a). But on Count 2, rotate CW 180 degrees before transferring your weight onto your right foot, which remains in place—this movement is like an about-face (see Figure b). It is extremely important to be sure that your hips are above your right foot and your weight is transferred forward onto the ball of your right foot exactly on Count 2, because any delay will cause you to be late on the cha-cha-cha portion that travels on Counts 3-and-4 "forward-forward-forward." Imagine that you now have your back to your partner.

To return to face your partner again, reverse your movements to place your right foot forward on Count 5 (see Figure c), rotate 180 degrees CCW, and shift your weight forward onto the ball of your left foot on Count 6 (see Figure d). Then continue traveling forward during the cha-cha-cha portion on Counts 7-and-8.

After any two half chases, the man has two options. If the man decides to continue the half chase, the woman will see his back. If he decides to end the half chase, the woman will be facing her partner again (see Figures e and f).

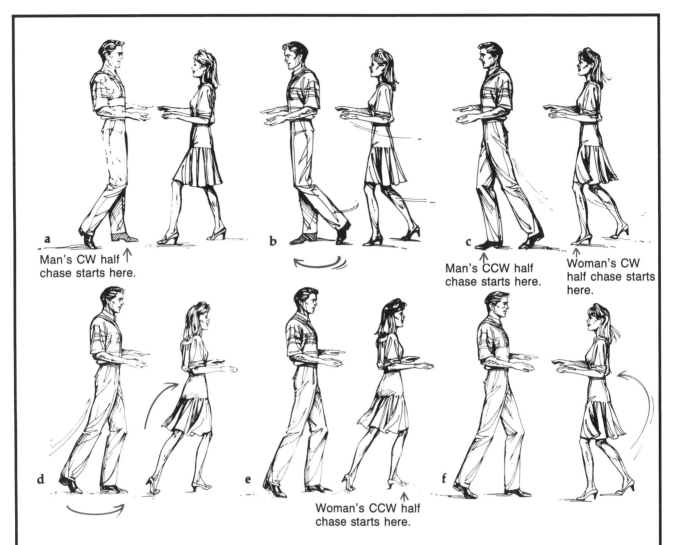

Man's CW half ↑
chase starts here.

Man's ↑ CCW half
chase starts here.

Woman's CW
half chase starts
here.

Woman's CCW half
chase starts here.

Notice that you must orient your turns (CW or CCW) according to your own midline (see Figure g). Imagine that your midline initially faces 12 o'clock. Thus, at separate times during the half chase, both partners alternately turn CW (from 12 o'clock to 6 o'clock) and CCW (from 6 o'clock back the same way to 12 o'clock).

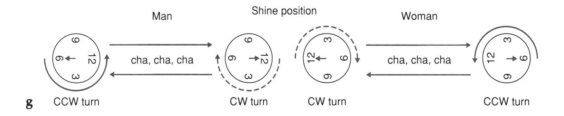

Success Goals = 4 correct repetitions of the half chase in each of the following ways: (a) without a partner or music; (b) with a partner and no music; and (c) with a partner and music

Your Score =

a. (#) _____ correct repetitions of the half chase (without a partner or music)

b. (#) ____ correct repetitions of the half chase (with a partner and no music)

c. (#) ____ correct repetitions of the half chase (with a partner and music)

2. Full Chase

The full chase is similar to the half chase, except that a full turn occurs. To execute the full turn, repeat the half chase directions for Counts 1 and 2. However, on Counts 3-and-4, continue to rotate CW during your small cha-cha-cha steps by rotating your toes CW a little bit with each step to complete another 180-degree turn. Try this without a partner or music.

Then try the full chase with a partner. The man does his full chase (instead of his forward-half basic step), while the woman does her regular backward-half basic step. Then, the man does his regular backward-half basic (facing his partner), while the woman does her full chase (instead of her forward-half basic step).

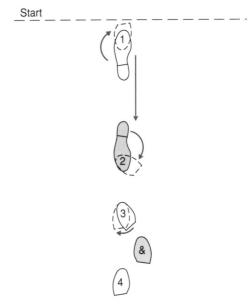

Full chase on forward half of cha-cha basic

Success Goals =4 correct repetitions of the full chase in each of the following ways: (a) without a partner or music; (b) with a partner and no music; and (c) with a partner and music

Your Score =

a. (#) ____ correct repetitions of the full chase (without a partner or music)

b. (#) ____ correct repetitions of the full chase (with a partner and no music)

c. (#) ____ correct repetitions of the full chase (with a partner and music)

3. Alternating the Full and Half Chase

Start facing a partner, and do the basic forward and backward cha-cha. Whenever the man's left foot is free (during the forward half of the basic), he can lead either the full chase or the half chase. This is a test for the woman to recognize what is to come next, and for the man to correctly time his nonverbal leads. The man can vary the order, the number of repetitions, and the number of basic cha-chas between each variation.

Success Goal = 4 different ways of alternating the half chase and the full chase, with a partner, to music, and with the appropriate styling and fluidity

Your Score = (#) ____ different ways of alternating the half chase and the full chase, with a partner, to music, and with the appropriate styling and fluidity

Drills for Cha-Cha Variations: Two-Hands Joined Position

For both of the following variations (the freeze and the push-away turns), continue to use the typical cha-cha styling characteristics, especially maintaining eye contact with your partner.

Both variations are appropriate options from a two-hands joined position with your partner. Politely ask a partner to help you practice each variation without music first.

4. Freeze

To execute the freeze variation, set up and lead as if you are going to do the basic cha-cha to both sides. Thus, partners should be facing the man's right side with inside hands joined (the man grasps the woman's palm between his thumb and fingers) and outside hands free and bent at 90-degree angles.

The freeze adds two more counts to the cha-cha basic's four counts. Just before Count 1, the man rotates his wrist and hand CW and lowers his hand below his waist (so that both partners' arms are straight). On Count 1, each partner steps to the side with the inside foot (see Figure a). On Count 2, the man bends his elbow to lift his partner's hand and arm above his waist as both partners transfer weight onto their outside feet (see Figure b), which remain in place (in a forward-backward stride position). Immediately repeat these two leads (Counts 3 and 4).

Then turn inward to face your partner for the cha-cha-cha steps that travel sideways (Counts 5-and-6).

Thus, think of a "down-up, down-up, cha-cha-cha" rhythm for the freeze leads to both sides. Do this with a partner without music. Once you both have the rhythm, try the freeze to music.

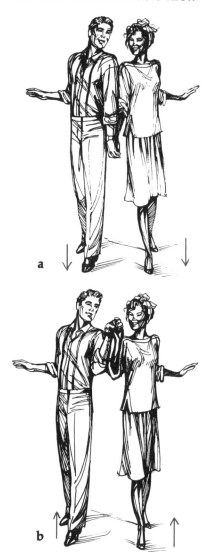

Success Goals = 4 correct repetitions of the freeze with a partner (a) without music, then (b) with music

Your Score =

a. (#) ____ correct repetitions of the freeze with a partner, without music

b. (#) ____ correct repetitions of the freeze with a partner, with music

5. Push-Away Turns

The push-away turns have numerous options and are a blend of the chase variations previously practiced. You can equate it to a three-quarters chase that starts facing the side, then rotates a three-quarters turn to face your partner.

Again, set up to face the man's right side, with inside hands joined (remember that the man grasps the woman's hand between his thumb and fingers—she does not literally "hold" his hand in the cha-cha). Just before Count 1, the man rotates his hand and wrist CW one quarter of a turn (see Figure a) and gently pushes and releases his partner's hand away from him (CCW) with a horizontal, "sweeping" motion (keeping his hand waist-high) (see Figure b).

As in the half chase, both partners rotate away from each other 180 degrees to end up with the weight on the outside foot on Count 2 (see Figure c). Then continue rotating another 90 degrees to face your partner prior to the cha-cha-cha steps that travel sideways (see Figure d). The woman needs to keep her elbows bent 90 degrees with her palms down, so that the man can easily regrasp both of her hands during the sideward cha-cha-cha steps.

This push-away turn variation can be executed on the opposite side by reversing the previous descriptions. Remember that the side steps need to be repeated in multiples of 2. Thus, if you do one push-away turn variation, then you need to do at least one other basic step, which could be either another push-away turn variation on the opposite side or a plain side basic.

The man has many options for when to give the lead for the push-away turn variation. Common options may include both single and multiple repeats. Do at least four consecutive side basics, and try each of the following examples with a partner (first without music, then with music):

* Turning only on the first side basic
* Turning only on the second side basic

a

b

c

- Turning only on the third side basic
- Turning only on the fourth side basic
- Turning on both the first and second side basic
- Turning on both the third and fourth side basic
- Turning on all four side basics

Success Goals = 2 correct repetitions of each of the 7 push-away turn options (a) without music, then (b) with music

Your Score =

a. (#) _____ correct repetitions of each of the 7 push-away turn options, without music

b. (#) _____ correct repetitions of each of the 7 push-away turn options, with music

6. *Alternating the Freeze and Push-Away Turns*

Experiment with your partner to randomly alternate the freeze and the push-away turn variations. The man can vary the order, the number of repetitions, and the number of basic cha-chas between each variation. At first it is helpful to repeat at least twice whichever variation is selected, so that your partner can have more time to identify the lead differences between these variations in the two-hands joined position.

Repeat these variations with your partner to music. Notice that the main differences in the leads are in the height of the man's hand, as follows:

- A waist-high hand moving directly to the side signals a side basic.
- A waist-high hand moving directly to the side with a push and release signals a push-away turn.
- A hand moving below, then above, the waist signals a freeze.

Success Goal = 4 different ways of alternating the push-away turns and the freeze with a partner, to music and with the appropriate styling and fluidity

Your Score = (#) _____ different ways of alternating the push-away turns and the freeze with a partner, to music and with the appropriate styling and fluidity

Drill for Cha-Cha Combination Options

7. *Two-Position Combinations*

Problem-solve with your partner to create at least four different cha-cha sequences that include at least one variation appropriate in the shine position and at least one variation appropriate from the two-hands joined position. Add the appropriate transitions and use any order and any number of repetitions. Work for smooth transitions, and add appropriate styling throughout.

Here is one example that you might try:

- Start moving forward and backward in the shine position—four times.
- Do a half chase—four times.
- Repeat forward and backward in the shine position—four times.
- Move into the two-hands joined position.
- Give a lead to move sideways.
- Do two push-away turns (one on each of the next two side steps).
- Do two more sideward basics.
- Make transitions to forward and backward directions and to shine position again.

What are some other ways to combine cha-cha variations in the shine and the two-hands joined positions? Can you substitute a different variation from each position? Can you vary the number of repetitions of a particular step? Can you vary the total number of steps combined? Can you repeat your sequence twice in a row? See the Cha-Cha Combination Options Chart for a summary of your options.

Cha-Cha Combination Options Chart

Shine Position Variations	Two-Hands Joined Position Variations
1. Half chase	1. Freeze
2. Full chase	2. Push-away turn(s)

- Only on the first side basic
- Only on the second side basic
- Only on the third side basic
- Only on the fourth side basic
- On both the first and second side basic
- On both the third and fourth side basic
- On all four side basics

Success Goals = 3 continuous repetitions of each of 4 different cha-cha sequences to music, using both shine and two-hands joined position variations, with fluidity and styling

Your Score = (#) _____ continuous repetitions of each of 4 different cha-cha sequences to music, using both shine and two-hands joined position variations, with fluidity and styling

Sequence 1: _____

Sequence 2: _____

Sequence 3: _____

Sequence 4: _____

Circle the number of the sequence that works best for you.

Step 9 Fox-Trot Variations and Combination Options

You practiced fox-trot two-combination leads in Step 6. (Review these if you need to before proceeding with this step.) Now you are ready to combine three or more variations into fluid sequences that travel CCW around the perimeter of the room whenever traffic is not impeded by other couples. Basically, the man has two types of variations to choose from, stationary or traveling, depending on the particular situations encountered on the dance floor.

You may have noticed that a set routine is easiest to practice. However, once you know how to execute a number of fox-trot variations and are ready for an evening of dancing, it is advisable to vary your routines (the ways you combine the variations), because a set routine does not take into account other couples on the dance floor. For example, if your set routine alternates two box steps (stationary variation) and two magic steps (traveling variation), but another couple moves immediately in front of you and blocks your forward motion just as the magic step should be executed, then what do you do? If you don't have enough space to move in, you won't be able to continue the flow of motion that is characteristic of the fox-trot styling, and you might have to stop and start your set routine again. An alternative solution, when forward motion is blocked, would be to substitute another stationary variation (e.g., a left box turn or a repeat of the box step) until your CCW path is open again.

The new options in Step 9 include three more stationary variations (the magic rock, magic rock quarter turn, and cross step) and one more traveling variation (which combines two quarter-turns left followed by two quarter-turns right), from which you can now incorporate the backward variation of the half-box progression to permit CCW travel. The man's ultimate challenges are to survey, to anticipate, to select the appropriate variation (with the goal of traveling CCW whenever feasible), to give good leads, and to smoothly connect all possible variations into a flowing, consecutive sequence that blends both magic and box rhythms. The woman's ultimate challenges are to recognize the various leads, to know when the leads may be given, and to respond to the leads (without anticipating or leading) with the appropriate actions and stylings. Through problem solving, you will find that certain variations fit together better than others.

Drills for Fox-Trot Variations and Combination Options

1. *Combining Three Variations*

The purpose of this drill is to combine three variations that alternate either one or two of the stationary variations with either one or two of the traveling variations learned so far. Do two consecutive repetitions of each of the following three-variation combinations with a partner to fox-trot music.

a. Combinations composed of one stationary variation and two traveling variations include the following:

- Two boxes, four half-box progressions forward, four magic steps
- Two boxes, four magic steps, four half-box progressions forward
- One left box turn, four half-box progressions forward, two magic steps
- Two left box turns, two magic steps, six half-box progressions forward

b. Combinations composed of two stationary variations and one traveling variation include the following:

- One box, one left box turn, six magic steps
- Two boxes, one left box turn, eight half-box progressions forward
- One left box turn, two boxes, four magic steps
- Two left box turns, two boxes, four half-box progressions forward

c. Select any four out of the previous eight combinations to repeat, using a different number of repetitions with at least two of the three variations selected. Notice that repeating a variation at least two times gives you more time (with the exception of the left box turn, because it incorporates four quarter-turns). At some point, you will not need as much time and can more easily execute fewer repeats. Which combinations (and number of repeats) work best for you? Remember to add the appropriate styling and to feel the music.

Success Goals =

a. 2 consecutive repetitions of each of 4 3-variation sequences that combine 1 stationary variation and 2 traveling variations

b. 2 consecutive repetitions of each of 4 3-variation sequences that combine 2 stationary variations and 1 traveling variation

c. List 2 3-variation sequences (out of 4) that work best for you

Your Score =

a. (#) _____ repetitions of each of 4 3-variation sequences that combine 1 stationary variation and 2 traveling variations

b. (#) _____ repetitions of each of 4 3-variation sequences that combine 2 stationary variations and 1 traveling variation

c. Sequence 1: _____

   Sequence 2: _____

2. Magic Rock

Until now, you have used the magic rhythm only with a traveling variation. However, there are two stationary variations that also use a magic rhythm, the magic rock and the magic rock quarter turn. Both stationary variations use six counts, as does the magic step.

To execute the magic rock, imagine that you are beginning a magic step forward, but another couple comes in front without warning. Thus, on Counts 1 and 2, the man steps forward with his left foot (with a long, gliding reach), but because someone is in the way, he holds his right palm firmly (at the end of Count 2) to signal no more forward motion. On Counts 3 and 4, he pulls gently toward his own midline to rock his weight back onto his right foot (on Count 4, the ball of his left foot briefly touches the instep of his right foot). The usual ''side, close'' steps are taken on Counts 5 and 6. Thus, the following cues for the man match each whole count of the music: ''forward, hold, back, touch, side, close.''

The woman reverses the man's magic rock footwork actions to reach back with her right foot (Counts 1 and 2), becomes aware of the man's palm limiting further backward motion (Count 2), rocks her weight forward onto her left foot (Count 3), brings the ball of her right foot briefly beside the instep of her left foot (Count 4), then steps to her right side (with a shoulder-width step on Count 5), and closes (on Count 6). The following cues for the woman match each whole count of the music: ''back, hold, forward, touch, side, close.''

Notice that the magic rock variation moves you and your partner inward toward the center of the CCW circle. Thus, to use this variation, you will need to be on the outside of the circle and to limit the number of consecutive repetitions.

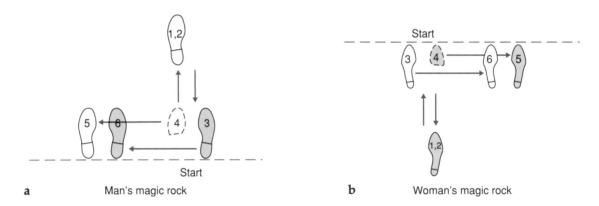

a   Man's magic rock   b   Woman's magic rock

Success Goals = 4 correct repetitions of the magic rock variation (a) without a partner or music, then (b) with a partner and music

Your Score =

    a. (#) _____ correct repetitions of the magic rock variation, without partner or music

    b. (#) _____ correct repetitions of the magic rock variation, with partner and music

3. Magic Rock Quarter Turn

The only difference between the magic rock and the magic rock quarter turn is that a CCW quarter turn is added to the latter during Counts 3 and 4. The CCW quarter turn is executed with the weight on the ball of the foot (the man's right foot, the woman's left foot) and is accomplished by twisting the toes 90 degrees. The man's lead on the quarter turn comes from rotating his entire upper torso (shoulders and arms together) CCW on Count 3.

Do four consecutive magic rock quarter turns, and you'll end up back where you started—just as you did in the left box turn.

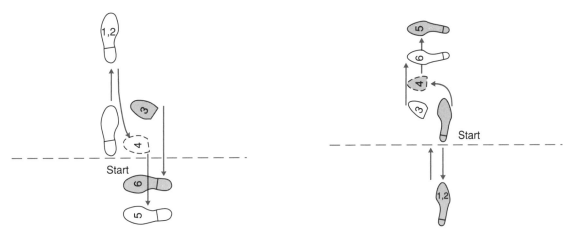

a   Man's magic rock quarter turn   **b**   Woman's magic rock quarter turn

Success Goals = 4 correctly executed magic rock quarter turns (a) without a partner or music, then (b) with a partner and music

Your Score =

a. (#) _____ correctly executed magic rock quarter turns, without a partner or music

b. (#) _____ correctly executed magic rock quarter turns, with a partner and music

4. Squaring the Corners

Another option is possible with the magic rock quarter turn that can help you orient yourself to the four walls of the room. If you do only one magic rock at a time, you make a sharp 90-degree turn that can be used at each of the four corners of the room. This option allows you to make a CCW *rectangular* path, rather than a CCW circular path, around the perimeter of the room, which is especially helpful early in the learning process.

Try the following alternating (ABAB) sequence with a partner, to fox-trot music: Use the magic step (A) to travel the length of the room, then do one magic rock quarter turn (B), continue with the magic step (A) for the width of the room, do one magic rock quarter turn (B), and continue repeating this alternating sequence.

Success Goal = 2 complete CCW rectangular paths (alternating the magic step with 1 magic rock quarter turn at each of the 4 corners)

Your Score = (#) _____ complete CCW rectangular paths (alternating the magic step with 1 magic rock quarter turn at each of the 4 corners)

5. Two Left Quarter Turns and Two Right Quarter Turns

You will feel as if you are opening and shutting a door as you execute two left quarter turns, then two right quarter turns. The secret is to have your arms and shoulders in a proper frame, such that your entire upper torso rotates either CCW or CW. To "open the door," start as if you are doing a left box turn, but only do half of it (two quarter-turns). As usual, the man twists his upper torso and frame CCW prior to any Count 1.

With the man's back to the CCW line of direction (LOD), the man pulls his right palm slightly toward his midline and reverses his upper torso twist to a CW direction (to "shut the door"). This new action facilitates either a toe-in position (with the man's left foot) or a toe-out position (with the woman's right foot), which must be taken on a 45-degree angle. Finish the rest of the basic fox-trot's "touch, side, close" during the first, right quarter turn, and continue a CW torso twist for the second, right quarter turn (the man's right foot toes out, and the woman's left foot toes in), which brings you back to the original starting position. If you do not progress in the LOD, you are probably overrotating your shoulders and stepping beyond a 45-degree angle.

When working with your partner, be aware that the shoulders and upper torso indicate which direction to turn in, and they also tell you (nonverbally) which foot should toe in or toe out. Also notice that this is a traveling variation.

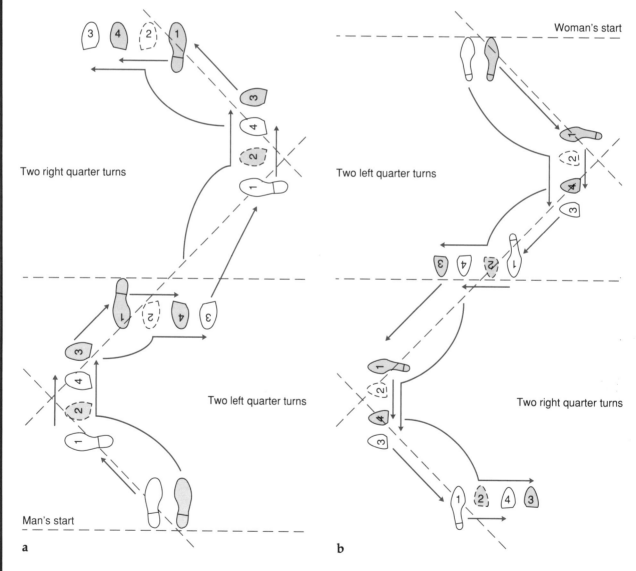

Success Goals = 4 correct repetitions combining 2 left quarter turns and 2 right quarter turns (a) without a partner or music, then (b) with a partner and music

Your Score =

a. (#) ＿＿＿ correct repetitions of 2 left quarter turns and 2 right quarter turns (without a partner or music)

b. (#) ＿＿＿ correct repetitions of 2 left quarter turns and 2 right quarter turns (with a partner and music)

6. Adding a Half-Box Progression Backward

Now you can opt to "sandwich" the half-box progressions backward *between* the two left quarter turns and the two right quarter turns. Adding any even number of repetitions of the half-box progression backward also makes this a traveling variation.

After the two left quarter turns, the man does not immediately rotate CW, but keeps his shoulders perpendicular to the LOD and reaches backward with his left foot to begin the half-box propressions backward (remember to alternate feet as the man reaches back with his "left, touch, side, close," then with his "right, touch, side, close"). At the end of any even number of repetitions of the half-box progressions backward, the man can rotate his upper torso CW to signal the upcoming two right quarter turns. Again, avoid any tendency to overrotate your shoulders or feet, which limits traveling.

Because the man travels backward, he must be sure that the CCW direction is clear. If there is too much traffic, he may opt not to execute the half-box progressions backward. Then, when there is a free path to execute this variation, the man may look over one shoulder as he moves backward to monitor traffic. Also, the woman may help warn him (verbally or nonverbally) whenever an unexpected couple crosses the man's intended path.

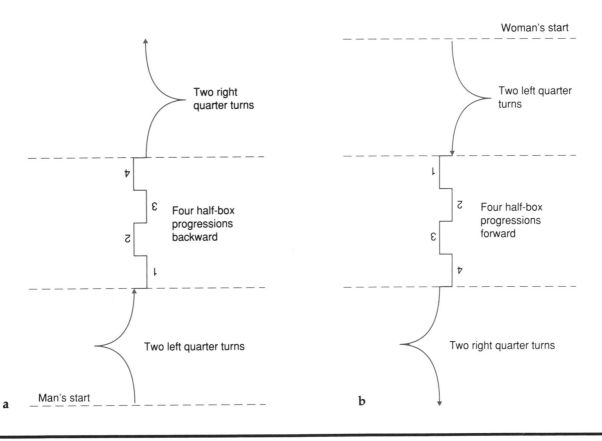

Success Goals = 4 correct repetitions of the "sandwich" combination (a) without a partner or music, then (b) with a partner and music

Your Score =

   a. (#) _____ correct repetitions of the "sandwich" combination (without a partner or music)

   b. (#) _____ correct repetitions of the "sandwich" combination (with a partner and music)

7. Cross Step

A fancy, stationary variation is the cross step, which occurs during the second half of a box step. Begin the forward half-box as usual, except twist (the man's left foot, the woman's right foot) 45 degrees on Count 4 to face both the inside of the CCW circle and your extended arm (to be in a semiopen position). The lead into this semiopen position results from the man rotating his shoulders and upper torso CCW 45 degrees on Count 4, but keeping his hands in their same position. Try this subtle rotation first without, then with, a partner.

During the cross portion (the second half-box), bend your pushoff knee to take a long cross-step with your inside foot (the man's right, the woman's left). This bend lowers your height and must be smoothly executed. At the end of Count 2, twist back (on your inside foot) to face your partner again (to be in closed dance position) as you bring your outside foot beside the arch of your inside foot (during the "touch"). Then continue with your usual "side, close" steps. The following cross-step cues match each whole count of the music: "forward (man), touch, side, twist; cross, touch (twist), side, close." Notice that this variation moves inward (to the man's left) like the magic rock.

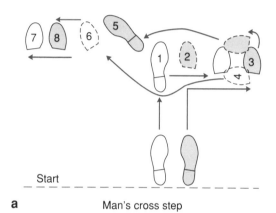

a   Man's cross step

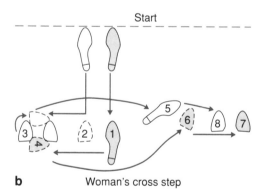

b   Woman's cross step

Success Goals = 4 correct repetitions of the cross step (a) without a partner or music, then (b) with a partner and music

Your Score =

   a. (#) _____ correct repetitions of the cross step (without a partner or music)

   b. (#) _____ correct repetitions of the cross step (with a partner and music)

8. *Combining the Cross Step*

Because the cross step uses box rhythm, it combines well with other box rhythm variations. Do two repetitions of each of the following two-variation combinations to fox-trot music, and add appropriate styling:

a. Box step
   Cross step
b. Half-box progression forward
   Cross step
c. Two left quarter turns and two right quarter turns
   Cross step

Make sure that your transitions between variations are fluid. Which one of the three combinations is composed of stationary (rather than traveling) variations?*

Success Goal = 2 consecutive repetitions of each of the 3 previous combinations to music, with fluidity and styling

Your Score = (#) ____ consecutive repetitions of each of the 3 combinations to music, with fluidity and styling

---

*The answer is sequence a.

9. *Combining Four Stationary Variations*

If the dance floor is very crowded and you cannot travel forward, you can opt to do any of the stationary variations you know so far. Thus, you have five choices:

- Box step
- Left box turn
- Magic rock
- Magic rock quarter turn
- Cross step

Politely ask a partner to dance, and create at least four different sequences that combine any four stationary variations. You may vary both the order and the number of repetitions of each. Notice which sequence flows most easily for you and your partner.

Success Goal = 4 different sequences (combining any 4 stationary variations) to music, varying both the order and the number of repetitions, with fluidity and styling

Your Score =

Sequence 1: _____

Sequence 2: _____

Sequence 3: _____

Sequence 4: _____

Circle the number of the sequence that flows most easily for you.

10. Combining Four Traveling Variations

If the dance floor is not crowded, the ultimate fox-trot goal is to travel in the LOD. You now have four traveling variations to select from:

- Half-box progressions forward
- Two left quarter turns followed by two right quarter turns
- Magic step forward
- Sandwich option (two left quarter turns, any even number of half-box progressions backward, two right quarter turns)*

Politely ask a partner to dance, and create at least four different sequences that combine these four traveling variations. You may vary both the order and the number of repetitions of each. Notice which sequence flows most easily for you and your partner.

Success Goal = 4 different sequences (combining 4 traveling variations) to music, varying both the order and the number of repetitions, with fluidity and styling

Your Score =

Sequence   1: _____

Sequence   2: _____

Sequence   3: _____

Sequence   4: _____

Circle the number of the sequence that flows most easily for you.

---

*May substitute magic steps backward for the half-box progressions backward.

11. Mixing Stationary and Traveling Variations

Rarely will you be able to do either all stationary or all traveling variations on the dance floor. Therefore, you need to be able to mix both stationary and traveling variations to most appropriately fit the flow of traffic.

Politely ask a partner to dance. Create at least five different sequences of any five variations that mix both stationary and traveling variations. Use any order and any number of repetitions of each. Notice which sequence flows most easily for you.

Success Goal = 5 different sequences (mixing any 5 stationary and traveling variations) to music, varying both the order and the number of repetitions, with fluidity and styling

Your Score =

Sequence   1: _____

Sequence   2: _____

Sequence   3: _____

Sequence   4: _____

Sequence   5: _____

Circle the number of the sequence that flows most easily for you.

12. Spontaneous Sequences

Assume that you are dancing on a crowded dance floor. This means that the man must survey the other couples and select and lead the appropriate stationary or traveling variations to best fit the situations encountered. The woman must be ready to respond to the man's lead, to execute all variations automatically, to smoothly make transitions, and to add the fox-trot styling characteristics.

Continue to experiment with a partner until you feel that you can smoothly connect at least six variations into fluid sequences that reflect the fox-trot's styling and that connect with the music. Use any number of repetitions, and include both magic and box rhythm options in your stationary and traveling variation selections. The Fox-Trot Combination Options Chart summarizes the fox-trot variations you may select from.

Fox-Trot Combination Options Chart

Stationary Variations

A. Magic rhythm options

1. Magic rock
2. Magic rock quarter turn

B. Box rhythm options

1. Box step
2. Left box turn
3. Cross step

Traveling Variations

A. Magic rhythm options

1. Magic step forward
2. Magic step backward

B. Box rhythm options

1. Half-box progressions forward
2. Two left quarter turns and two right quarter turns
3. Half-box progressions backward
4. Sandwich combination

Success Goals =

a. Spontaneous sequences of at least 6 different fox-trot variations, with fluidity and styling, for the length of 6 different songs

b. List your favorite 6-variation combination order

Your Score =

a. _____ Spontaneous sequences of at least 6 different fox-trot variations, with fluidity and styling, for the length of 6 different songs (yes or no)

b. Variation 1: _____

Variation 2: _____

Variation 3: _____

Variation 4: _____

Variation 5: _____

Variation 6: _____

Step 10   Polka Variations and Combination Options

So far, you know the polka leads for traveling forward in two different positions (inside-hands joined position and semiopen position) and the transitions to continuously alternate these positions. If you need to refresh these skills, review the polka drills in Step 6. Otherwise, you are ready to add one variation in both of these positions and to explore the resulting combination options.

Drills for Polka Variations and Combination Options

1. Underarm Turn

Grouping your polka basic steps in multiples of four, the underarm turn (UAT) variation is a CW turn only for the woman on the fourth polka basic. Start with inside hands joined, and let them swing freely back before taking your first polka basic. Do three polka basics with arm swings, and momentarily freeze with both inside hands back (see Figure a). The UAT lead occurs just before and during the fourth polka basic.

To execute the lead for the UAT, the man separates his fingers and extends two fingers for the woman to loosely grasp. Hands swing forward as normal, except that the man continues to lift his hand higher than his partner's head (see Figure b). Keeping his first two fingers pointing downward, he then draws a small half circle CW in the air over his partner's head. This lead turns the woman under the man's arm in a CW direction as she takes her fourth polka basic (see Figure c). The man does his fourth polka basic in place. At the end of the turn, the man must keep his hand back, in preparation for repeating the next group of four polka basics (see Figure a again).

Success Goals =

a. 8 repetitions of the UAT variation (without music)

b. Continuous repetition of the UAT variation for the length of one song

Your Score =

a. (#) _____ repetitions of the UAT variation (without music)

b. _____ Continuous repetition of the UAT variation for the length of 1 song (yes or no)

2. *CW Turn With Partner*

This variation involves both partners turning together as a unit. It is a very difficult variation when done continuously, yet it is extremely fun to do and represents the ultimate polka variation that most people want to see, learn, and do. You have already practiced this CW turn and spotting without a partner, so now it's time to work with a partner.

Take a few seconds to glance straight forward, toward the right wall, and toward the left wall. You will need these points of reference when you execute the CW turn variation with your partner.

For this variation, your polka basics are also grouped in fours (two forward and two turning). Start in a semiopen position with your partner. Do two polka basics forward, with outside arms firmly extended forward (see Figures a and b).

On the third polka basic, the man lowers the outside arms, lifts the inside elbows to shoulder height to create an imaginary diagonal line, and travels CW 45 degrees in front of his partner to face his original right wall (see Figure c). The woman needs to take small, in-place steps on her third polka basic. Check that both partners have their weight on their outside feet at the end of this third basic polka. To lead during the hop and a 45-degree turn at the end of his third polka basic, the man must pull his right palm and fingers both CW and inward on the woman's back.

On the fourth polka basic, the man continues to rotate CW 45 degrees, taking small, in-place steps until he faces his original left

a

b

wall, while the woman rotates CW 45 degrees to move in front of her partner. The man lifts the extended arms high in the back and lowers the elbows in front to again create an imaginary diagonal line toward the front (see Figure d). The remaining 45-degree rotation to face the original front occurs on the hop at the end of the fourth basic. The man's lead includes pulling his right palm and fingers both CW and inward on the woman's back as he brings the extended arms to the front and holds them firm and straight—to signal that the turn is over (see Figure a again).

As you refine this variation, both partners can reinforce the illusion of the imaginary diagonal line toward the front by looking down it during each part of the turn.

Alternately do two polka basics forward and two polka basics turning with your partner at least eight times without music, then for the length of one slow song.

c

Success Goals =

a. 8 repetitions of the CW turn (alternating 2 basics forward and 2 basics turning) with partner (without music)

b. Continuous repetition of the CW turn (alternating 2 basics forward and 2 basics turning) with partner for the length of 1 slow song

Your Score =

a. (#) ____ repetitions of the CW turn with partner (without music)

b. ____ Continuous repetition of the CW turn with partner for the length of 1 slow song (yes or no)

d

3. Two-Position Transition Sequence

Continuously repeat the following two-position transition sequence (from the polka drills in Step 6), and feel free to vary the number of times in a row that you repeat the polka basic. Work for smoothness, especially on the transitions, and blend each of the following parts into a continuous sequence:

- Inside-hands joined position
- Transition to semiopen position

- Semiopen position
- Transition to inside-hands joined position

Do this two-position transition sequence at least four times consecutively without music, then repeat it with slow polka music. Make sure that your free hands are on your hips when you are in the inside-hands joined position.

Success Goals = 4 consecutive repetitions of the 2-position transition sequence (a) without music and (b) with music

Your Score =

a. (#) _____ consecutive repetitions of the 2-position transition sequence (without music)

b. (#) _____ consecutive repetitions of the 2-position transition sequence (with music)

4. Add the UAT to the Sequence

Continue to repeat the two-position transition sequence from the previous drill, and add the UAT variation in some way during the inside-hands joined position. For example, you can alternate the UAT with polka basics as follows:

- Three basics forward, then the UAT on the fourth basic
- Five basics forward, then the UAT on the sixth basic
- **Follow the general rule**: Do the UAT on any even-numbered basic

Add the UAT to the two-position transition sequence in two different ways by varying the number of basics prior to the UAT. Repeat each way at least twice to slow polka music. Make sure that the entire sequence remains continuous.

Success Goals =

a. List 2 different ways of adding the UAT to the 2-position transition sequence

b. 2 consecutive repetitions of both ways of adding the UAT to the 2-position sequence (with music)

Your Score =

a. (#) _____ basics prior to UAT (version 1)

   (#) _____ basics prior to UAT (version 2)

b. (#) _____ consecutive repetitions of both ways of adding the UAT to the 2-position transition sequence (with music)

5. Add the CW Turn With Partner to Sequence

Repeat the two-position transition sequence (from Drill 3), and add the CW turn with partner in some way during the semiopen position. For example, you can vary the number of basics executed forward and turning, as follows:

- Two basics forward and two basics turning (to complete one CW turn)
- Four basics forward and two basics turning (to complete one CW turn)
- Four basics forward and four basics turning (to complete two CW turns)
- **Follow the general rule**: Alternate any even number of repetitions of each

Add the CW turn with partner to the two-position transition sequence in two different ways by varying the number of basics executed forward and turning. Repeat each way at least two times to slow polka music. Make sure that the entire sequence remains continuous.

Success Goals =

a. List 2 different ways of adding the CW turn with partner to the 2-position transition sequence

b. 2 consecutive repetitions of both ways of adding the CW turn with partner to the 2-position sequence (with music)

Your Score =

a. (#) _____ basics forward and (#) _____ basics turning (version 1)

   (#) _____ basics forward and (#) _____ basics turning (version 2)

b. (#) _____ consecutive repetitions of both ways of adding the CW turn with partner to the 2-position transition sequence (with music)

6. *Spontaneous Sequences*

Politely ask a partner to dance. Assume that you are dancing on a crowded dance floor, and select the polka variation appropriate for the traffic flow. For example, if there are other couples immediately in front of you and your partner (blocking your forward motion), then the man can

- lead any of the variations used in the inside-hands joined position,
- do only forward polka basics in the semiopen position, or
- shorten the length of each step taken.

If there are no other couples immediately in front of you and your partner, then the man also has the option of leading the CW turn with partner in the semiopen position (i.e., the man can lead any variation in either position).

Create at least six different two-position transition sequences that include both the UAT variation and the CW turn variation in some way. You can use any number of polka basics and any order. Make sure that your actions are appropriate for the flow of traffic encountered.

Success Goal = Spontaneous 2-position transition sequences that include both the UAT and the CW turn with partner in some way and that are appropriate for the flow of traffic for the length of 6 different songs

Your Score = Spontaneous 2-position transition sequences that include both the UAT and the CW turn with partner in some way and that are appropriate for the flow of traffic for the length of (#) _____ different songs

Step 11 Waltz Variations and Combination Options

You have practiced two-combination leads in Step 6. (Review the waltz drills if necessary before proceeding with this step.) Now you are ready to combine three or more waltz variations into fluid sequences that travel CCW around the perimeter of the room whenever traffic is not impeded by other couples. However, once you and your partner are on a dance floor with other couples, you will find that the flow of traffic is random and unpredictable, just as it is for the fox-trot and polka. Thus, the man must constantly survey the other couples' locations and adjust his sequences according to the same two types of situations (and challenges) previously encountered: stationary and traveling variations. If another couple is immediately in front, the man can opt to do any one of the stationary waltz variations. If another couple is not immediately in front, the man can opt to do any one of the traveling waltz variations.

The new options in Step 11 include one more stationary variation (the cross step) and one more traveling variation (which combines two quarter-turns left followed by two quarter-turns right); from the latter you can incorporate the half-box progressions backward to also permit CCW travel. You may recognize these step names, because they are exactly the same variations that were used in the fox-trot. Two main differences are that the waltz variations use *only* box rhythm options and that all waltz variations are executed in 3/4 time (instead of the fox-trot's 4/4 time).

Drills for Waltz Variations and Combination Options

1. Combining Three Variations

The purpose of this drill is to combine three waltz variations into a sequence that alternates either one or two stationary variations with either one or two traveling variations. Do two consecutive repetitions of each of the following three-variation combinations with a partner to waltz music:

- Two boxes, four half-box progressions forward, two left box turns
- Two boxes, one left box turn, four half-box progressions forward
- One left box turn, four half-box progressions forward, two boxes
- Two left box turns, two boxes, six half-box progressions forward

Notice that repeating a variation at least twice gives you more time (except for the left box turn, which incorporates four quarter-turns). At some point, you will not need as much time and can more easily execute fewer repeats. Remember to take a longer first step by bending your pushoff foot, and to group your footwork actions in threes with each whole count of the music. Which two of the above sequences involve stationary, then traveling, then stationary movement?*

Then assume that you are dancing on a crowded dance floor. Use this alternating pattern to create at least three different three-variation sequences. Vary the number of repetitions and/or the order. Make sure that your sequences are consecutively executed and appropriately selected to fit the flow of traffic encountered.

Success Goals =

a. 2 consecutive repetitions of each of the listed 3-variation sequences (with partner to music)

b. 3 different 3-variation sequences appropriate for the flow of traffic (varying the number of repetitions and/or order) for the length of 3 different waltz songs

Your Score =

a. (#) _____ consecutive repetitions of each of the listed 3-variation sequences

b. (#) _____ different 3-variation sequences appropriate for the flow of traffic for the length of 3 different waltz songs

_____

*The answers are the first and third sequences.

2. Two Left Quarter Turns and Two Right Quarter Turns

You will feel as if you are opening and shutting a door as you execute two left quarter turns, then two right quarter turns. The secret to leading this variation properly is to have your arms and shoulders in a proper frame, such that your entire upper torso rotates either CCW or CW. To "open the door," start as if you are doing a left box turn, but only do half of it, or two quarter-turns. As usual, the man twists his upper torso and frame CCW prior to any Count 1.

With the man's back to the CCW line of direction (LOD), the man pulls his right palm slightly toward his midline and reverses his upper torso twist to a CW direction (to "shut the door"). This new action facilitates either a 90-degree toe-in position (with the man's left foot) or a 90-degree toe-out position (with the woman's right foot). Count 1's step is taken on a 45-degree angle. Finish the rest of the waltz basic's "side, close" during the first, right quarter turn, and continue a CW torso twist for the second, right quarter turn (the man's right foot toes out 90 degrees, the woman's left foot toes in 90 degrees). This brings you back to the original starting position. If you do not progress forward toward the LOD, you are probably over-rotating your shoulders and stepping beyond a 45-degree angle. Do at least four correctly timed and executed repetitions combining two left quarter turns and two right quarter turns without a partner or music.

When working with your partner, be aware that the shoulders and upper torso indicate which direction to turn in, and they also tell you (nonverbally) which foot should toe in or toe out. Make sure that a correct torso twist occurs before Count 1, and that the quarter-rotation steps (either forward or backward) are correctly taken on a 45-degree angle during each Count 1 of the 3/4-time music. Do at least four correctly timed and executed repetitions combining two left quarter turns and two right quarter turns, with a partner, to waltz music.

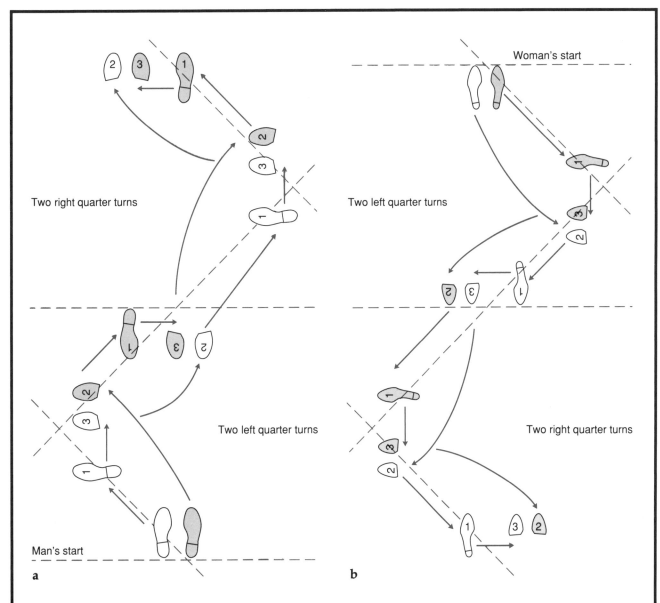

Two right quarter turns

Two left quarter turns

Two left quarter turns

Woman's start

Two right quarter turns

Man's start

a

b

Success Goals =   4 correctly timed and executed repetitions combining 2 left quarter turns and 2 right quarter turns (a) without a partner or music, then (b) with a partner and music

Your Score =

a. (#) ____ correctly timed and executed repetitions of 2 left quarter turns and 2 right quarter turns (without a partner or music)

b. (#) ____ correctly timed and executed repetitions of 2 left quarter turns and 2 right quarter turns (with a partner and music)

3. Adding Half-Box Progressions Backward

Now you can opt to ''sandwich'' the half-box progressions backward *between* the two left quarter turns and the two right quarter turns. This combination permits you to travel forward in the LOD. Thus, after the two left quarter turns, the man does not immediately rotate CW, but keeps his shoulders perpendicular to the LOD and reaches backward with his left foot to begin the half-box progressions backward (the woman must remember to alternate feet as the man reaches back with his "left, side, close," then with his "right, side, close"). At the end of any even number of repetitions of the half-box progressions backward, the man can rotate his upper torso CW to signal the upcoming two right quarter turns. Again, avoid any tendency to overrotate your shoulders or feet (beyond 45 degrees), which limits traveling.

Because the man travels backward, he must be sure that the CCW direction is clear. If there is too much traffic, he may opt not to execute the half-box progressions backward. Then, when there is a free path to execute this variation, the man may look over one shoulder, as he moves backward, to monitor traffic. Also, the woman may help warn him (verbally or nonverbally) whenever an unexpected couple crosses the man's intended path.

Do at least four correctly timed and executed repetitions of this "sandwich" combination without a partner or music. Then repeat with a partner to waltz music. Make sure that the torso twists are timed correctly before the first count of the two CCW and the two CW quarter turns, yet that shoulders remain square during the half-box progressions backward.

Success Goals = 4 correctly timed and executed repetitions of "sandwich" combination (a) without a partner or music, then (b) with a partner and music

Your Score =

a. (#) _____ correctly timed and executed repetitions of "sandwich" combination (without a partner or music)

b. (#) _____ correctly timed and executed repetitions of "sandwich" combination (with a partner and music)

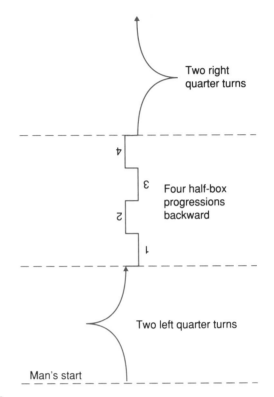

a

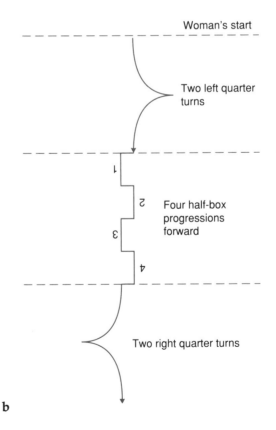

b

4. Four-Variation Combinations

At this point, you know two stationary and three traveling variations for the waltz. The purpose of this drill is to practice combination options involving four different variations. Do at least two consecutive repetitions of each of the following four-variation combination examples with a partner to music:

- Two boxes, four half-box progressions forward, two left quarter turns and two right quarter turns, left box turn
- Two boxes, two left quarter turns and two right quarter turns, left box turn, eight half-box progressions forward
- Two boxes, four half-box progressions forward, left box turn, two left quarter turns and two right quarter turns
- Four half-box progressions forward, "sandwich" combination, two boxes
- Two boxes, left box turn, two left quarter turns and two right quarter turns, four half-box progressions forward

Now, feel free to modify the above combinations by varying the number of repetitions or using a different order. Select any four variations that best fit the flow of traffic encountered while dancing with a partner for three different waltz songs. Keep all transitions smooth.

Success Goals =

a. 2 consecutive repetitions of each of the listed 4-variation sequences (with a partner and music)

b. 3 different 4-variation sequences appropriate for the flow of traffic (varying the number of repetitions and/or order) for the length of 3 different waltz songs

Your Score =

a. (#) _____ consecutive repetitions of each of the listed 4-variation sequences (with a partner and music)

b. (#) _____ different 4-variation sequences appropriate for the flow of traffic for the length of 3 different waltz songs

5. Cross Step

The cross step is a fancy, stationary variation in the waltz. Like the fox-trot cross step, the cross portion is executed during the second half of a box step, but the waltz's timing is much faster. Thus, execute a forward half-box as usual, and twist with the outside foot (the man's left foot, the woman's right foot) 45 degrees after bringing the feet together on Count 3. This rotates you and your partner to face both the inside of the CCW circle and your extended arms (in a semiopen position). The

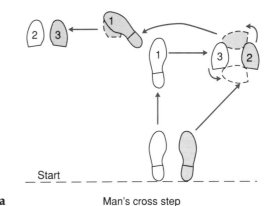

a　　　　Man's cross step

lead into this semiopen position results from the man rotating his shoulders and upper torso CCW 45 degrees on Count 3 while keeping his hands and arms in their same position. Do this subtle rotation first without a partner or music.

To add styling during the cross portion (second half-box), bend your pushoff knee (outside knee) to take a long cross-step with your inside foot (the man's right, the woman's left). This bend lowers your height and must be smoothly executed. On Count 2, twist back (on the inside foot) to face your partner again (in closed dance position) and step to the side. Close on Count 3. The following cross-step cues (for the man) match each whole count of the music: "forward, side, close-and-twist; cross, twist-and-side, close."

Do at least four repetitions of two consecutive cross steps with your partner to waltz music. Notice that this variation moves you both inward (to the man's left, to the woman's right) toward the center of the circle.

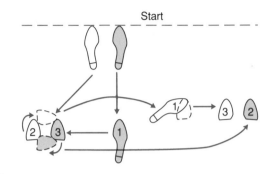

b Woman's cross step

Success Goals = 4 correctly timed and executed repetitions of 2 consecutive cross steps (a) without a partner or music, then (b) with a partner and music

Your Score =

a. (#) ____ correctly timed and executed repetitions of 2 consecutive cross steps (without a partner or music)

b. (#) ____ correctly timed and executed repetitions of 2 consecutive cross steps (with a partner and music)

6. Combining the Cross Step

The purpose of this drill is to combine the cross step with one other variation. Do each of the following combinations at least twice with a partner to music:

- Two box steps, two cross steps
- Two half-box progressions forward, two cross steps
- Left box turn, two cross steps
- Two left quarter turns and two right quarter turns, two cross steps

Which combination flows best for you and your partner?

With a partner, use any modification of the above combinations to include a cross step in two different sequences to two different waltz songs. To increase the dramatic effect with the cross-step variation, both partners should look toward their extended arms when in the semiopen position. Notice that multiple repetitions of the cross step take you and your partner toward the center of the room. Therefore, be sure that no one is in your way and that you are on the outside of the room before leading multiple cross steps.

Success Goals =

a. 2 consecutive repetitions of each of the listed 2-variation combinations (with a partner and music)

b. 2 different sequences smoothly modifying any 2 of the listed combinations, with a partner, to 2 different songs

Your Score =

a. (#) ____ consecutive repetitions of each of the listed 2-variation combinations (with a partner and music)

b. (#) ____ different sequences smoothly modifying any 2 of the listed combinations, with a partner, to 2 different songs

7. Spontaneous Sequences

Politely ask your partner to dance. Imagine that you are on a crowded dance floor. Experiment with combining at least five waltz variations in a random order and with any number of repetitions for the length of one song. Select appropriate stationary and traveling variations to fit the traffic flow. The following Waltz Combination Options Chart summarizes the two types of waltz variations that you may select from. Repeat this process until you can smoothly react to the flow of traffic without hesitation for the length of six different songs. Make sure that you add appropriate styling and fluidity.

Waltz Combination Options Chart

Stationary Variations	Traveling Variations
1. Box step	1. Half-box progression forward
2. Left box turn	2. Two left quarter turns and two right quarter turns
3. Cross step	3. Half-box progression backward
	4. Sandwich combination

Success Goals = Spontaneous sequences of at least 5 different waltz variations, appropriately and fluidly repeated with correct styling for 6 different songs

Your Score = ____ Spontaneous sequences of at least 5 different waltz variations, appropriately and fluidly repeated with correct styling for the length of 6 different songs (yes or no)

Step 12 Expanding Your Dance Options

Now that you know the basic steps, transitions, variations, and sequence options for five dance styles, you are ready to go beyond the packaged steps to create your own dance steps, transitions, variations, and routines (set sequences). These creative challenges require problem solving, which takes time. So don't expect yourself to have an immediate idea or to have an immediately polished sequence or routine. However, there are certain guidelines, reflecting the decision-making stages built into the previous steps, that can inspire your creativity. These guidelines, typical "problems" to solve, and sample solutions will be presented in the drills.

WHY IS IT IMPORTANT TO EXPAND YOUR DANCE OPTIONS?

Obviously, the more "perfect" practice you have, the more polished your dance skills can become. So survey your community to locate places where you can practice your new dance skills. You will need to be flexible, to adapt to these varied dance settings.

The purpose of this step is to give you ideas for adapting your styling and basic steps to fit the dance situations you may encounter. For example, what styling, basic step, and variation options do you have if you want to dance to folk, country, or contemporary music? Which social dance variations most easily transfer to these different situations? How do you adapt to very slow music? What variations can you do in the polka to stay within a spot (because there is usually restricted travel at a wedding or on a very crowded dance floor)? How do you create a new basic step or a demonstration routine? You can address all of these questions by using the knowledge you acquired in Steps 1 to 11 to create new options and opportunities to dance. The most important goal is to work in unison with your partner to create fluid, appropriate, and continuous sequences that fit the music.

Drills for Expanding Your Dance Options

1. Dancing to Contemporary Music

If you want to transfer your ballroom basics to contemporary music, listen closely to the music and mentally try one of three basics to the music: swing, cha-cha, or fox-trot. Try out on the dance floor each basic step that you think fits the music, and decide which fits it best.

Once you have selected a basic step that best fits the music, continue to experiment, while dancing, with all the variations you know so far, adapting them to best fit the available floor space and number of other couples dancing. Let yourself feel the music, to modify your styling to best flow with the music. Try to keep your sequences continuous.

Continue to follow these procedures until you find three different contemporary songs to accompany your swing, fox-trot, and cha-cha basics and combinations.

Success Goal = Correctly match swing, fox-trot, and cha-cha basics to 3 contemporary songs

Your Score = (#) _____ correct matches

2. Dancing to Country or Folk Music

Repeat the previous drill, except now experiment with the basics for swing, polka, or waltz, to find out which of these three best fits the type of music (country or folk) being played. Again, your style will change with this music. Watch others on the dance floor, and try to imitate their actions.

Once you find a basic step that matches the music, continue to experiment, while dancing, with all of the variations you know so far, and feel free to modify the basics. Notice that the country two-step is the triple step (or the polka basic without a hop on the upbeat). Shoulders and torso leans are more common with country music. If you use the double-lindy basic, you might experiment with a touch (to either the side or beside the ball of your other foot) before stepping (on Counts 2 and 4).

Success Goal = Correctly match swing, waltz, and polka basics to 3 different country or folk songs

Your Score = (#) _____ correct matches

3. Dancing to Very Slow Music

When very slow 4/4-time music is played, you could select the most appropriate existing variations, or problem-solve to adjust or create new variations. To give you a better idea of how versatile these options are, try to solve the following fox-trot problems (sample solutions are provided):

Problem a: Which existing fox-trot variations best lend themselves to very slow music?

Sample solution a: Start by trying all of the variations you know so far. In particular, try the following variations, using all of the available time to make your motions fluid and connected with the music:

- Box step
- Left box turn
- Cross step
- Magic rock, in place
- Magic rock quarter turns

Problem b: How could you do the magic rock not only in place, but also side to side (rather than forward and backward) and still maintain the magic rhythm? What would you do?

Sample solution b: You might try leaning (swaying) to the man's left (Counts 1 and 2), then leaning (swaying) to the man's right (Counts 3 and 4), and continuing with the regular ''side, close'' (Counts 5 and 6), or add an action for your free foot during Counts 2 and 4, as follows: side, touch, side, touch, side, close.

Problem c: The previous solution works well on a crowded floor, but it still takes you to the man's left. How can you modify this new side-step variation to rotate either CW or CCW?

Sample solution c: Remember how you rotated in the swing? Try that same procedure here: Start by rotating one eighth of a rotation either before each Count 1 or only on Counts 5 and 6 ("side, close" steps); then gradually continue to rotate on all steps. Work for smoothness on all direction changes.

Problem d: How would you incorporate a half turn (by modifying the half- and full-chase variations from the cha-cha) into the fox-trot to create a fancy, pivoting turn with your partner?

Sample solution d: Imagine a doughnut or tire inner tube shape on the floor with both an inner and an outer circle (see Figure a). Both partners always step with the left foot on the outer circle and with the right foot on the inner circle. The pivot results from pushing with the outer circle's foot and advancing the heel of the inner circle's foot CW. (This is called a *buzz step* in square dancing.)

The lead requires the man to move forward toward his partner, apply pressure on her back, and join right hips. Timing for the man is advance and pull, then step on the outer circle with his left foot (Count 1 is shown in Figure b), and pivot (Count 2 is shown in Figure c). Timing for the woman is to be pulled closer, then step on the inner circle (Count 1), and pivot (Count 2).

Once you can do a half turn with your partner, continue to add more half turns until you have at least a six-count pivot turn (three half turns). This fancy solution gives you more variety and more timing options, because the pivot turns can also be executed faster than the slow tempo being played. Try the pivot turn with either fox-trot or swing music.

a   b   c

Success Goal = Effectively demonstrate solutions to at least 2 out of 4 problems presented

Your Score = (#) _____ solutions effectively demonstrated

4. Creating In-Place Polka Variations

Most of the polka variations so far have been traveling options. What do you do if there is restricted room to travel in the LOD? Try each of the following suggested variations, then feel free to create your own.

Sample variation a. If you have approximately 5 to 10 feet of space in which to move left or right, try this heel-and-toe variation. In a semiopen dance position, start with outside feet (man's left; woman's right), and do the following: heel (see Figure a), toe (see Figure b), heel, toe, slide, slide, slide, and change weight to your outside foot on the fourth slide; then repeat to the opposite side.

Sample variation b. If you only have a few feet of space in which to move forward at a time, then try this heel-and-toe variation that incorporates the polka basic. Start side by side with your partner, hook inside elbows, and place outside hands on hips. Both partners start with the left foot and do the following actions:

Part A

Counts 1 and 2: Left heel-dig forward, and step in place (see Figures a, b)

c d

Counts 3 and 4: Right toe-dig backward, and touch in place (see Figures c, d)

e f

Counts 5 and 6: Right heel-dig forward, and step in place (see Figures e, f)

g h

Counts 7 and 8: Left heel-dig forward, and cross in the air (see Figures g, h)

Part B

Counts 1 to 8: Four polka basics (forward)
Double-check that you are hopping *only* on the upbeat during the polka basics forward. Once you get the feel of these actions, accent the heel portions (in Part A) by leaning back slightly (approximately 45 degrees), and accent the toe portions (in Part A) by leaning slightly forward (approximately 45 degrees).

Success Goals =

a. Continuous execution of sample variation a, using proper head and frame accents, for the length of 1 polka song

b. Continuous execution of sample variation b, using proper body accents, for the length of 1 polka song

Your Score =

a. ____ Continuous execution of sample variation a, using proper head and frame accents, for the length of 1 polka song (yes or no)

b. ____ Continuous execution of sample variation b, using proper body accents, for the length of 1 polka song (yes or no)

5. Creating a New Basic Step

A basic step is composed of two or more locomotor movements that blend to create a rhythmic pattern. Try the sample solution, then use the following "Challenge" guidelines to create your own dance sequence, if you feel comfortable doing so:

Challenge	Sample Solution
a. Combine two locomotor movements.	a. Three walks and a hop (schottische).
b. Decide on position with partner.	b. Inside hands joined.
c. Decide which foot to start with.	c. Outside feet.
d. Decide what directions to move in (keep in multiples of 4).	d. Forward and backward, forward and backward (A); side and side, side and side (B)
e. Vary the basic step somehow.	e. Four step-hops with a kick to each side (crossing midline) (C).
f. Vary the direction and partner position.	f. Four step-hops while rotating in place away from your partner (men CCW, women CW) (D).
g. Repeat entire sequence (ABCD), and add arms to somehow relate to partner.	g. Keep inside hands joined and touch (clap) outside hands on each schottische hop.

If the previous basic step feels familiar to you, that is because you experimented with an abbreviated version of this schottische sequence in Step 3, Drill 7.

Success Goal = Correctly demonstrate the sample solution to 4/4-time music

Your Score = ____ Correctly demonstrated the sample solution (yes or no)

6. Creating a Demonstration Routine

You might take two different approaches to creating a demonstration routine. Some dancers prefer to plan a constant sequence that never varies. Other dancers prefer to have some favorite combinations and vary the order. I feel that the latter approach introduces the element of surprise, because both dancers have to be ready for any possible combination. Try both approaches with the following challenge situation, and decide for yourself.

Challenge	Sample Solution
a. Decide on a specific beginning that fits the music.	a. Both partners start 10 feet apart in a pose. In unison, mirror a turn with your partner to 4/4-time music. Take triple steps toward each other.
b. Decide on a middle that fits the music.	b. As you and your partner meet, revolve around each other until you can both start the triple-swing basic. Continue with selected swing combination options (relate to your partner as much as you can with arm, head, and eye movements).
c. Decide on an end that fits the music.	c. One partner poses on a high level and the other poses on a low level—for instance, the woman sits on the man's knee, and each lifts an arm high (hold the final pose 3 to 4 seconds).

If you have trouble getting your routine started, experiment with using a theme to give you inspiration and help you remember what comes next. For example, one of my students imagined himself as Fred Astaire walking casually down the street, tipping his hat to his dance partner, inviting her to dance, sharing her company (spinning, rotating), and thanking her for the dance. Sometimes the music can be inspirational because it lends itself to a particular style or type of movement, which can be accentuated or exaggerated.

Success Goal = Create a fluid routine of any length that has a definite beginning, middle, and ending, with the music

Your Score = ____ Demonstrated a routine to solve the above challenge (yes or no)

Rating Your Total Progress

You have covered a lot of material in this book. In particular, you have explored rhythm and timing elements, and you have learned basic steps, how to communicate with your partner verbally and nonverbally, and how to use your new dance skills in various situations. Take time to evaluate your progress by completing the following charts.

RHYTHM AND TIMING

Foundational skills include knowing when to move with the music and what part of your foot connects with which count of the music to create a continuous rhythmic pattern. Rate yourself on your abililty to do the following:

	Very good	Good	Fair	Poor
Identify time signatures	_____	_____	_____	_____
Identify the downbeat/upbeat	_____	_____	_____	_____
Connect footwork to the music	_____	_____	_____	_____
Demonstrate locomotor movements (e.g., walk, hop, skip, or gallop) to a rhythm	_____	_____	_____	_____
Modify and combine locomotor movements to form basic steps, including these:				
a. Triple lindy (swing)	_____	_____	_____	_____
b. Cha-cha	_____	_____	_____	_____
c. Magic step (fox-trot)	_____	_____	_____	_____
d. Single lindy (swing)	_____	_____	_____	_____
e. Polka	_____	_____	_____	_____
f. Box step (fox-trot)	_____	_____	_____	_____
g. Box step (waltz)	_____	_____	_____	_____
h. Double lindy (swing)	_____	_____	_____	_____
(Man) Signal leads prior to the downbeat	_____	_____	_____	_____
(Woman) Respond to leads (without anticipation)	_____	_____	_____	_____
Move in unison with partner to music	_____	_____	_____	_____

STYLING AND FLUIDITY

How you move (your styling) is critical for adding both flavor and variety to your basic steps. Styling includes adding appropriate characteristics that fit the style of the dance and the music. How smoothly you move (fluidity) is critical for blending the various partner positions together so that you can have a continuous, free-flowing dance sequence with your partner and the music. Rate yourself on your ability to do the following:

	Very good	Good	Fair	Poor
Stand in proper alignment	_____	_____	_____	_____
Move with proper alignment (carriage)	_____	_____	_____	_____
Maintain appropriate arm positions (holding own weight instead of letting gravity take over)	_____	_____	_____	_____

Make smooth transitions between the following partner positions:

a. Swing

Semiopen position

	Very good	Good	Fair	Poor
to one-hand joined position	_____	_____	_____	_____
to two-hands joined position	_____	_____	_____	_____
to semiopen position	_____	_____	_____	_____

b. Waltz

Closed dance position

	Very good	Good	Fair	Poor
to semiopen position	_____	_____	_____	_____
to closed dance position	_____	_____	_____	_____

c. Fox-trot

Closed dance position

	Very good	Good	Fair	Poor
to semiopen position	_____	_____	_____	_____
to closed dance position	_____	_____	_____	_____

d. Cha-cha

Shine position

	Very good	Good	Fair	Poor
to two-hands joined position	_____	_____	_____	_____
to one-hand joined position	_____	_____	_____	_____
to shine position	_____	_____	_____	_____

e. Polka

Inside-hands joined position

	Very good	Good	Fair	Poor
to semiopen position	_____	_____	_____	_____
to CW turns	_____	_____	_____	_____
to semiopen position	_____	_____	_____	_____
to inside-hands joined position	_____	_____	_____	_____

| Select variations to best fit situations(s) encountered on the dance floor | _____ | _____ | _____ | _____ |

	Very good	Good	Fair	Poor
Consistently demonstrate characteristic styling points with partner for the following dance styles:				
a. Swing	_____	_____	_____	_____
b. Waltz	_____	_____	_____	_____
c. Fox-trot	_____	_____	_____	_____
d. Cha-cha	_____	_____	_____	_____
e. Polka	_____	_____	_____	_____
Smoothly blend variations into sequences with partner to music	_____	_____	_____	_____

ETIQUETTE AND CONFIDENCE

Additional benefits to social dancing come from the pleasant interchanges and experiences you share with your dance partner. Practicing proper etiquette rules can increase your popularity (and confidence) both on and off the dance floor. Rate yourself on your ability to do the following:

	Very good	Good	Fair	Poor
Implement appropriate etiquette rules (e.g., thank your partner)	_____	_____	_____	_____
Project a positive attitude (in mind and body)	_____	_____	_____	_____
Move with precision and poise	_____	_____	_____	_____
Move in unison both with your partner (instead of doing your own thing) and with the music	_____	_____	_____	_____
Smile	_____	_____	_____	_____

OVERALL SUCCESS

In general, how do you feel about your overall progress at this point?

____ Very successful

____ Somewhat successful

____ Fairly successful

____ Unsuccessful

Now look over all of your previous ratings and identify not only your strong points, but also those points that may need a little more practice. Place a star beside your three strongest points, and circle your three weakest points. Decide how you can improve any weak areas. Start by reviewing the appropriate section(s) in this book. Then, go out and dance!

Glossary

accents—Beats in the music that are emphasized.

alignment—Correct body posture while standing stationary. From a side view, visualize an imaginary plumb line aligning with the ear, shoulder, hips, knees, and ankles.

ball-change—Two weight changes, first stepping back, then forward, from the ball of one foot onto the other foot.

ballroom dance—A partner dance typically done in a ballroom.

broken rhythm—A combination of slow and/or quick beats that takes more than one measure.

carriage—Correct alignment of body parts while moving.

close—To bring the free foot beside the supporting foot and transfer weight onto it.

closed position—A position in which partners face each other with shoulders parallel, the woman slightly to the man's right, elbows curved away from the body, and partners touching as follows: The man's right palm and fingers are below the woman's left shoulder blade; the man holds the woman's right hand in his left hand; and the woman curves her left arm on top of the man's right arm, with her curved, left hand resting in front of his right shoulder.

dance basics—The traditional combination of locomotor movements universally associated with a particular dance style ("packaged").

downbeat—The first count of any measure.

even rhythm—Steady, consistent steps or counts, each getting the same time value.

free foot—The foot without any weight on it.

inside foot—The foot closest to your partner.

inside-hands joined position—A side-by-side partner position with the woman on the man's right, the man holding the woman's left hand in his right hand.

line of direction (LOD)—An imaginary line that refers to the flow of traffic, which is counterclockwise around the perimeter of the room.

locomotor movements—Actions that transport you from one location to another—the walk, run, leap, jump, hop, skip, gallop, slide, and so forth.

measure—The number of beats grouped together according to the time signature.

outside foot—The foot farthest away from your partner.

phrase—Two or more measures grouped together.

quick step—The rhythmic length of a step. It is usually one count, but it can be quicker relative to other beats. (Not to be confused with an advanced dance basic called the "quick step," which is not covered in this book.)

rhythmic pattern—A recurring series of beats and/or actions.

schottische—A combination of three walking steps and a hop.

semiopen position—A variation of the closed dance position, with a 45-degree-angle body rotation toward the extended arms.

shine position—A facing position, or challenge position, with partners standing approximately 2 feet apart without touching and with shoulders parallel.

slow step—The rhythmic length of a step. It is usually two counts, but it can be slower relative to other beats.

social dance—A partner dance done for recreational purposes.

spot dance—A dance done within a small area on the floor (as opposed to traveling in the LOD).

step—A transfer of weight from one foot to the other.

supporting foot—The foot with weight on it.

tempo—The speed of the music.

time signature—The number and duration of beats in a measure.

triple step—Three steps taken to two beats of the music (an uneven rhythm).

two-step (country)—Continuous triple steps with torso leans to either side; the polka basic without a hop.

underlying beats—The number of beats per measure, usually apparent in the drumbeat in music.

uneven rhythm—A combination of both whole and half steps or counts (slow and quick beats) in a recurring pattern.

upbeat—The last beat of a measure, which is often called an "and" count when starting to move with the music.

Individual Program

INDIVIDUAL COURSE IN _____ GRADE/COURSE SECTION _____

STUDENT'S NAME _____ STUDENT ID # _____

SKILLS/CONCEPTS	TECHNIQUE AND PERFORMANCE OBJECTIVES	WT* X	POINT PROGRESS** =				FINAL SCORE***
		%	1	2	3	4	

Note. From "The Role of Expert Knowledge Structures in an Instructional Design Model for Physical Education" by J.N. Vickers, 1983, *Journal of Teaching in Physical Education*, **2**(3), p. 17. Copyright 1983 by Joan N. Vickers. Adapted by permission.

*WT = Weighting of an objective's degree of difficulty.

**PROGRESS = Ongoing success, which may be expressed in terms of (a) accumulated points (1, 2, 3, 4); (b) grades (D, C, B, A); (c) symbols (merit, bronze, silver, gold); (d) unsatisfactory/satisfactory; and others as desired.

***FINAL SCORE equals WT times PROGRESS.

About the Author

Judy Patterson Wright is an accomplished dancer who has taught social dance at the junior high, high school, and college levels since 1971. She earned her PhD in 1981, her dissertation focusing on the process of learning a waltz sequence. She has taught many styles of dance, as well as physical education methods, activities, and classes in motor development and behavior.

Dr. Wright's dance experience includes a wide variety of styles—ballroom and social dance, tap dance, jazz, modern dance, ballet, folk dance, square dance, country western dance, and aerobic dancercise. Judy and her husband, Sam Wright, are popular instructors who specialize in progressive teaching methods. They have participated in country western dance competitions since 1992, dancing the two-step, waltz, cha-cha, east-coast swing, west-coast swing, and polka. As a couple they have won numerous regional and national competitions, and through their company, Wright Way Productions, they have produced 12 instructional videotapes for country western dance couples.

Honored as one of the Outstanding Young Women of America in 1982, Dr. Wright has been repeatedly recognized as an Excellent Teacher at the University of Illinois at Urbana-Champaign. She has presented at the local, state, and national levels for many organizations, including two she belongs to, the American Alliance for Health, Physical Education, Recreation and Dance and the National Teachers Association for Country Western Dance Teachers.

Dr. Wright created the format for the Steps to Success Activity Series. Each book applies the latest research in an integrated manner, providing a continuum of skills and concepts sequenced to make learning easy.